CORVETTE

1963-1967

(THIRD EDITION)

LARRY M. GALLOWAY

To order additional copies of this book, contact:
Xlibris
844-714-8691
www.Xlibris.com
Orders@Xlibris.com

ISBN: Softcover   978-1-6641-8839-6
         EBook   978-1-6641-8840-2

Print information available on the last page

Rev. date: 10/15/2021

DEDICATION

This book is dedicated to all of the wonderful people I worked with at Chevrolet St. Louis, Chevrolet Central Office, Detroit and DowSmith, Ionia, Michigan. Many are mentioned in this book by name and title. There are many more whose names escape me that are not listed.

I was an employee of General Motors from August 16, 1962 until May 9, 1969. My interface with many people inside and outside of General Motors was very positive and rarely had a moment of dissatisfaction or disappointment.

CONTENTS

CHAPTER 1

✦ ✦ ✦

DESIGNING A NEW CORVETTE

Design of the all new 1963 Corvette began many years before 1963. The Corvette that was finally released was the result of several years of prototype builds and market reviews. There were no design computers in the industry at that time so all drawings were manual, drawn by draftsmen.

The design drawings showing the styling were full scale on sheets of aluminum about one eighth inch thick painted white. Aluminum for ease of handling and painted white to give contrast to the lines. The lines were scribed into the aluminum to make them permanent. A design drawing displayed all of the lines that are visible and some not visible when you look at the vehicle. Since the drawing was full scale, the sheet of aluminum for a typical side view drawing of this type had to be about 200 inches long and 60 inches high as the 1963 Corvette is 175.3 inches long and 49.8 inches high. A typical body drawing did not include the wheels and tires, only the body.

The aluminum plate was scribed with lines five inches apart horizontally and vertically forming a grid. The drawing began from a "zero" inch horizontal height line from which all vertical dimensions were referenced. This line was close to the floor pan or underbody of the car. Dimensions below the line were negative and dimensions above the line were positive. A second vertical reference "zero" inch line was positioned at the front of dash. The dash panel on a body drawing is the panel below the windshield and behind the engine of a front engine car. The dash panel is sometimes called the toe pan because of the angle portion behind the clutch, brake and accelerator pedals. The dash panel is commonly called a fire wall from the days when an engine fire occurred, the dash panel or firewall protected the passengers. The firewall term is not used by most people because it implies an unsafe condition that is frowned upon by many, especially lawyers. The use and location of "zero" inch lines is likely a carry over practice from the days when Fisher Body designed and built all car bodies for General Motors. The parts of a car in front of the dash were car division responsibility and behind the dash were Fisher Body responsibility. Body dimensions in front of the vertical "zero" inch line were negative and those toward the rear were positive.

These design drawings did not have dimensions, only lines. All dimensions were obtained by scaling or measuring the drawing. Since they were full scale, with a grid of reference lines spaced at 5 inch intervals, all dimensions could be lifter or obtained with a 6 inch scale, usually with .010 inch divisions. As the drawings were on aluminum plates or sheets that expand or contract significantly with temperature change, the plates were stored at constant temperature. This storage requirement restricted the mobility of the drawings. So, when the drawings were finished and ready for release, a mylar plastic copy was made. Mylar is very durable, stable and portable. The mylar plastic drawings facilitated pencil dimensioning and sketching additions or deletions for ease of study as pencil lines could be easily washed off.

This kind of drawing looked like a side view of the Corvette but was a very busy drawing with many lines, some more or less parallel and many that crossed others. The untrained eye might see the image of the Corvette but not the detail that was presented. The top horizontal line on the drawing represented the very top of the body at the longitudinal center line of the body. The next line down represented a line 5 inches left or right of the center line. The third line down represented a line 10 inches left or right of the centerline, etc. until the entire width of the body was represented. The door and door opening lines that were more or less vertical were shown full scale just like they were to look on the finished car. Sections were "cut" at critical points to show the relationship of mating parts like the door to door opening. A section drawing represents a picture of the parts as if the parts were cut to see the ends of the cut parts. Sections are required to show the shape of parts and their relationship to other parts.

The long gentle flowing lines of the body were drawn manually using large "sweeps" or templates. The draftsman had many many "sweeps" to choose from, each slightly more or less curved to produce the line needed to represent the body flow. Sweeps could be up to several feet in length. Each longitudinal line on the drawing crossed a vertical 5 inch line at a specific height. This height point was taken from the full size styling clay model using conventional measuring equipment like a height gage at the desired point at a point 5 inches or 10 inches or 15 inches, etc. from the centerline.

This method of design was very labor intensive, slow and difficult to change. These aluminum "master" drawings were stored in a secure, temperature controlled room limiting their access.

Access to the mylar drawings was on a limited basis as many people wanted to use them and there were few copies. My department accessed these drawings only a few times during the production run of the 1963 Corvette. Everyone who worked on the Corvette at that time referred to the model as simply the "63 Model" for the entire 1963 through 1967 production run. The C1 or C2 etc. labels were not used and I do not know how or when that began.

Since there were no computer generated drawings, all parts and components for the body were designed using the aluminum or mylar body drawing as a reference for mating surfaces. Exterior moldings, for example, that were required to fit the sweep of the body were designed in "car position". Car position drawings show the part in the same position as if it were mounted on the body, sometimes with 5 inch body lines included for reference.

Part numbers were assigned manually in a system of paper records. General Motors had a system of even part numbers for the right side or right hand parts and odd part numbers for the left side or left hand parts. Many left and right hand parts were mirror images of each other. So one drawing, annotated, "left hand part symmetrically opposite except as noted" was common for identical left hand parts.

The "Bill of Material" (BOM) listed all of the part numbers required to build the Corvette. The BOM was a hierarchical listing. There was a part number for a complete, base, Corvette. Sub to that was a part number for each major component such as the body had a part number, the engine had a part number, etc. Under the body part number there would be part numbers released for the various assemblies, i.e., door assembly, hood assembly, seat assembly, etc. Under each assembly was listed all of the parts required to produce that assembly. Parts within the assembly, i.e., the door window lift mechanism, called a Window Regulator, had a part number and all of the parts within the Window Regulator had part numbers listed below the assembly part number. A 'part' is a single piece of the car, like a washer or a rivet. When two or more 'parts' are represented together or assembled, the part number represents an assembly.

When parts were released in different colors, like carpet parts or door trim panel parts, a chart was shown on the base assembly drawing showing a part number for that part in each color. Drawings of seats had part number charts showing a different part number for each color in vinyl and a different number for each color in leather.

The BOM was a very voluminous document, typically about 11 by 17 inches and 5 or 6 inches thick. Each page was numbered with a release date and change letter. All drawings showed the original release date and revision date and a revision letter, i.e, rev. a or rev. b, etc. Maintaining the BOM to the most current release date was a laborious process. When drawings were changed, and that happened often, the drawing files were maintained with the new drawing and the BOM was updated also. The Corvette Assembly Plant had one full time employee dedicated to maintaining these documents.

Service part numbers were often and usually different than production part numbers because parts for service usually were slightly different. Service parts or assemblies had different content so part numbers had to be different. For example, assemblies supplied for production may have more or less parts than a service part, i.e., the service part might include attaching hardware or threaded fasteners that the production part number would not include.

When a design change was made that affected the service part fit, form or function, the change would be designated "Coordinated Change" meaning that the serial number of the first car produced with the changed part required a notice to service. Service records were then amended to help the repairing dealer or part distributor supply the proper 'change level' part for cars before or after the changed part was introduced into the assembly process. The notice to service regarding this change was called a "Cut in Point" showing the date and serial number of the Corvette that the new part use began. This required control of all part inventory as any parts of the previous release could not be used after the Cut in Point. Parts of the previous release discovered after the cut in point were scrapped as their use would confound the service process. This sometimes happened and was often costly.

A change that required a cut in point became very significant when the body build by the outside supplier, DowSmith, began. Coordinating the Cut in Point of changes between the two plants was a constant problem. Coordinated changes were sometimes cut in at DowSmith before St. Louis and sometimes after St. Louis. The responsibility for maintaining service information belonged to St. Louis as that was the plant that shipped the Corvette to dealers. Consequently, some DowSmith bodies required rework by Chevrolet St. Louis to maintain continuity of the change. This created more work for the St. Louis Team and fueled the fire of discontent with the outsourced body.

Production parts were a source of parts for service, especially at the end of a model year run. The St. Louis Assembly plant typically received an order for service parts near the end of the production of each model year. Their quantities were estimates of parts required to service the model for 10 years. I am conservative, having grown up on a farm where every asset is saved "just in case" we needed it. I recall my first year when the Corvette plant inventoried parts that were not carry over for the 1964 model to fill service needs. For example, seat belts of each color were on hand after filling service requirements. There were hundreds, perhaps thousands of surplus and obsolete set belts remaining. Chevrolet scrap policy stated that "Parts being scrapped must be rendered not usable as originally intended". So, every surplus seat belt was placed over a metal scrap box about 4' by 4' square and struck with a heavy hammer cutting the belt into two pieces. I was shocked as the workmen performed this scrap process for days. Then, came the real shocker. The 1963 Corvette radio was a $250 option and service did not need many of the surplus radios. Since the 1964 Corvette Radio was different, the 63' radios in surplus inventory were scrapped. They were lined up on the factory floor and run over with a hi low. There were many parts that were scrapped but those two are indelible in my memory. Too bad we were not available to hold them for use today.

CHAPTER 2

+ ✦ +

CHEVROLET ST. LOUIS CORVETTE ASSEMBLY PLANT

St. Louis Corvette Assembly Plant

Chevrolet St. Louis Assembly Plant

The first 300 Corvettes were assembled in Flint, Michigan at the Chevrolet Pilot Plant. Corvette production for the 1954 model moved to St. Louis to a facility that was built about 1922 to house a kiln for drying wood for Chevrolet bodies of that era. John Evans was a Reliability Engineer on Corvette in St. Louis when I started working there as a Quality Analyst in August of 1962. He was involved with all quality meetings. He was also responsible for the interface between the plant and VIP visitors. When Doris Day's Corvette come off the line, John took note of the job and went over it to satisfy himself that she would be pleased. John and I spent many lunch hours together talking about the "Old Days".

John said that in the beginning, changes were initiated in St. Louis and documented in Detroit. A far cry from 1963 practices that did not allow any changes until after Product Engineering fully designed and tested the change before release. When a problem arose on the 1954 model, the change was developed by the resident Product Engineer in St. Louis and sent to Product Engineering in Detroit to be officially recorded. There were two Product Engineers resident in St. Louis throughout the Corvette build years of my tenure, John Schejbal and Bill Hart. The assembly plant had a lot of autonomy in the early days and when the V-8 engine came into production in 1955, John was there to solve the problems.

One of John's favorite stories involved the installation of the optional equipment Removable Hard Top on the assembly line. John observed the operator writing on the inspection card that the holes for attaching the hard top were in the wrong place. John ask the operator, "Who drilled the holes?" and the operator responded, "I did". John asked him what he was going to do about it and the operator said that he was going to repair and re-drill the holes as soon as he finished writing up the defect. John always got a good laugh telling this story to anyone he could find that had not heard it. His message was that they did not have the luxury of different people for inspectors and assemblers. He thought it comical that an operator would document his own defect and then repair it.

When the Corvette was introduced to Chevrolet Manufacturing they had been building trucks of all descriptions for years. The Corvette was the first total car, and a sport car to boot, that Chevrolet began to assemble. The car divisions, ie, Chevrolet, Buick, Pontiac, Cadillac and Oldsmobile historically built the chassis and the front fenders and hood and Fisher Body Division built the body. That is why there is one key for the doors and trunk and another for the ignition and glove box for cars through the 70's. The steering column, instrument panel and glove box was provided by the car division so they provided that key.

The 1963 Model Corvette offered the best of the best. The Corvette of these years offered a lot of options allowing the buyer to personalize his Corvette. The body design and styling also accommodated customizing. The Corvette in these years was affordable by many and insurance in those years was reasonable allowing ownership by a more youthful customer.

The 1963 Corvette body styling, heavily influenced by Bill Mitchell, the Head of GM Styling was used through the 1967 model year with only cosmetic changes. The most notable changes were in the front lower filler panel just behind the front wheels, the removal of the center divider in the back window and the hood simulated grills for 1964 and the addition of back up lights in the center at the rear for 1967. The seat styling also changed each year. Chassis, engine, driveline and suspension changed many times as well.

The 1963 Corvette design incorporated a metal structure making the body more rigid. The rigid body rattled less, doors fit and operated better and there were less water leaks.

Many terms used in the assembly of a car are created by the assembly operators. Corvette was no different. Every car, body or chassis was called a "job". I put parenthesis around the term the first time I use it and often there after. Many car companies continue to make statements like "Quality is Job One".

ST. LOUIS FACILITY

The Chevrolet St. Louis Assembly Plant was on the corner of Union Boulevard and Natural Bridge Avenue. The west wall of the building was moved some 40 or 50 feet west in 1963 to make more room for the new Corvette production. While digging the footings, the contractor, J. S. Alberici Construction who was always on site, found a buried rail road siding and furnace plumbing that was presumed to have been used for processing wood.

During World War II this building was used to build Amphibious DUKW known simply as "Ducks". (2.5 Ton 6 Wheel Amphibious Truck; D - Designed 1942; U - Utility; K - Front wheel drive; W - Two rear drive axles. 31 feet long 8 feet wide 24 troops.) There was a large water test trough in the middle of the plant used to test the "Duck" for water leaks. This test did not work well so the amphibians were driven to the Mississippi River for testing and repair where I understand some nearly sank.

When Corvette moved to the plant, one end of this trough was removed and filled to floor level and the remaining end was used for a ramp to drive hi-lows to and from the basement storage area. A salvage department was set up in the basement for the rework and salvage of defective parts.

The Corvette factory workers were a team of very proud workers, which they should be. They were building a very special and different automobile, a real American Sport Car.

They had build problems as any start-up experiences, especially in those days before quality was a really big issue. Aside from their own expertise, there was always "help" on hand or in the way from Chevrolet Central Office in Detroit. Everyone seemed to want to get involved with the Corvette.

I learned from people in the plant, as I worked there beginning August 16, 1962, that problems were solved in St. Louis followed by design changes in Detroit as needed.

BODY SHOP

The first station in the Body Shop was only a few feet from the last station in the Trim Shop. The Corvette body was built on a "body truck" just as all car bodies are or were built on "body trucks". The body truck creates a platform exactly like the car frame that the body will be mounted on to complete the car. The Corvette Assembly Plant was small as production was low. So, the Body Shop assembly line was a serpentine shape line beginning at the end of the Trim Shop and ending at the Paint Shop. The beginning of the Body Shop and the end of the Trim Shop lines were just across the main isle from the Body Drop station on the Chassis Line. This arrangement facilitated the return of the body truck from the end of the Trim Line to the beginning of the Body Shop line by hand. Most large assembly plants require a lengthy conveyor to return the body truck from body drop on the chassis line to the beginning of the body shop line. The Corvette tooling costs were also low as the assembly line design required a minimum number of body trucks.

Tapping plates and anchors, etc. were assembled to the underbody in the first station followed by placing the underbody on the body truck. All of the plastic body panels were FRP. The body truck provided accurate positioning of the underbody just as it would be set on the chassis later. Body truck dimensions were checked frequently with a large gage to assure proper height, front to rear and side to side location dimensions so the doors, hood and windshield would maintain their fits "as built" after installation on the chassis.

The Body Frame Assembly that provides the mounting surfaces and dimensional control for the body was nicknamed the "birdcage" by factory workers because the coupe body frame looked a little like a birdcage. Both the convertible and coupe birdcages were built in the same assembly fixture. The various parts of the bird cage were spot welded into sub-assemblies in separate fixtures and final assembled in the birdcage final assembly fixture. This design created an assembly that resulted in more consistent windshield and door openings than previous model years.

Door and window opening dimensional control is a major concern when building a high quality automobile. That is why current production automobiles use a single stamping to form the sides of the car. Some people refer to the assembly of a car body as "building holes". The door openings and windshield or back light "holes" or openings are critical. Other dimensions like fender heights, or front of car height are not so critical or noticeable as a oversize windshield or door opening.

The bird cage was made up of many parts and assemblies. When two or more parts are put together the result is an assembly. The windshield and door openings were made up of a frame that consisted of an inner and outer panel assembly creating a hat section. Many such assemblies were assembled together to form the windshield and door openings. Door and window dimensional variation was difficult to control and as a result door and windshield fit was affected. "Weldable sealer" was applied between many of the parts during the assembly process to prevent water leaks in the finished Corvette. Weldable sealer was a sealing material containing metallic particles that facilitated spot welding through the sealer creating a sealed union of the parts.

Following final welding of the bird cage, one or two Bird Cage Assemblies were checked per week in a special checking fixture to assure proper sizing of the windshield and door openings, the most critical part of the build. When bird cage dimensions varied, all the parts that were attached to it did not fit properly. After welding, the bird cage was cleaned by lowering it into a deep pit where a cleaner, I believe Carbon tetrachloride, at an elevated temperature was sprayed on the bird cage to clean it, stripping any manufacturing oil from the parts. This solvent dried quickly because of its elevated temperature and low boiling point. Thiokol sealer was applied in the rain gutter around the door opening of the coupe and painted with a zinc rich fuchsia color primer.

The bird cage was placed on the underbody followed by the attachment of bonding strips attached with pop rivets. Bonding strips were shot blasted to expose the glass fiber strands for better bond adhesion. All bonding surfaces of mating parts were also shot blasted for the same reason. The dash panel assembly, which included the fresh air plenum under the windshield, was assembled next.

The entire rear of the body was a subassembly which was assembled in an off-line fixture using bonding strips to hold the various panels together. The rear assembly consisted of the rear filler panel, left and right fenders and the coupe roof or convertible rear upper panel.

The body front assembly was built in a similar fixture and included more parts such as the front upper panel or hood opening panel, front wheel inner fender panels, radiator support or "horse collar" as the workers named it, headlamp supports, front support and fender lower front and rear filler panels. It may be interesting to note that the part of a car body that forms the part of the body that surrounds the wheels in the front are called fenders and in the rear are called quarter panels. Also, there is only one left or right side of a car. When the driver is in the driver's seat, his or her left side is the left side of the car.

Two operators built the Corvette body rear subassembly and assembled it to the underbody as a team. Two additional operators assembled the front end subassembly and bonded it to the hinge pillars and plenum or dash assembly in a similar manner as the rear. Tooling to locate the subassemblies was minimal. The body tooling did not locate the body panels to drawing specifications. The tooling simply held the panels in a position that was dependent upon the parts that the part was attached to. For example, the front fenders and upper panel was placed on the radiator support and plenum panels that, like all parts, exhibited variations that affected the overall height of the front of the Corvette. We inspected several complete bodies on a surface plate and the front of every body checked was .250 to .312 inches low to design.

The bond material consisted of 60% Resin, 32% Ground Asbestos Commercial Grade, 5% Catalyst (Benzol Peroxide) and 3% Promoter (Lamanac #400)[1]. The bond material was mixed at the time of use by an electrically controlled air driven mixing/dispensing head especially designed and built at Chevrolet St. Louis. A paper cone was rolled on a wood mandrel and taped much like a cake decorator uses only much larger. This cone held one or two quarts of bond material. Each operator filled a cone with bonding material and extruded it on the mating surfaces, one on each side of the line. The top of the cone was closed and held closed with one hand while the other hand was used to snip off the point forming a nozzle. The cone was then squeezed and manually guided to lay a bead of bond on the joint. The bonding material was exothermic and got hot enough to boil water when it set. The ratio of catalyst to resin regulated the time allotted for positioning and clamping the assembly, about 3 minutes to cure. That may seem like a long time but consider that the cure began when the bond material exited the mixing head. This was followed by applying the bond material to several feet of bond joint, a trip by the two operators to pick up the body assembly half and return to the line where they accurately positioned the body half by hand and clamped the assembly in place using clamps that assisted in location. Weather conditions also effected cure rate and sometimes operators had difficulty accomplishing the assembly before the bond cured or "went off" as they said. Bond material began curing the instant the mixing took place. These operators could bond a sub assembled front or rear body assembly to the mating surfaces on the job in 10 minutes, line speed at 6 per hour.

Following the body assembly, an epoxy filler was used to bond the coupe door rain gutter to the lock pillar just above the lock striker area. The 1/4 inch space between the top of the FRP lock pillar and the bird cage was also filled with epoxy on most 1963 coupe bodies. This practice was eliminated in late 1963 because a crack always appeared between the epoxy and the metal and customers thought that a structural failure was eminent. The open joint was eventually thought to look cleaner.

The lock and hinge pillar to outer panel joint was filled with bonding material. This operation was called "buttering-up" in the plant because the bond was spread like butter into the area. The body was completely dry sanded at this point in preparation for door and hood fit.

Both the convertible and coupe doors were assembled, dry sanded and hung in the body shop followed by the hood. No hood support yet, we held them up with a fixture, a broom stick I believe. FRP is subject to resin rich areas that crack because of a lack of fiberglass reinforcement. FRP is also subject

1 *Corvette Paint Finishing System* by R. H. Grosbeck, February 25, 1963 Detroit Section, Society of Plastic Engineers, Reinforced Plastic Group

to resin poor areas which are structurally weak and won't cover with paint. These areas, along with pits in the bond joint were repaired with bond material and sanded at this time.

We now have what is called a "body in white" in the industry because it has no paint and because a metal body without paint appears white.

PAINT SHOP

The body was heavily primed and baked next. The baking caused air trapped in the bonding material to expand and make holes in the joints which had to be ground out and filled again. These pits were the body shop's nemesis. They fought this problem for the entire build. The bodies were wet sanded with fine sandpaper and water to achieve a smooth surface for painting. Bodies were frequently rerun through the prime-bake-wet sand cycle until a satisfactory bond joint was achieved.

Following the acceptance of the primed body, the body was color coated with an acrylic lacquer. The paint on metal bodies is reflowed by raising the body temperature to a point that the paint almost melts and flows to provide a high gloss without polishing. The FRP panels of the Corvette will not tolerate this high temperature so the paint cannot be reflowed and must be polished after curing. Following the color coat, hood striping and black out paint was applied to the engine compartment, wheel wells, etc. as required.

The paint ovens baked the primer and sealer paint 30 minutes at a temperature of 250° F. The second color coat was baked 30 minutes at 200° F.[2] When the body exited the paint oven, an operator pulled the body, manually, to an area for masking and black out painting. This was the hottest job in the plant and I often wondered how the guys took the heat, especially in the St. Louis Summer.

TRIM SHOP

The trim shop or department was where most hardware and electrical items were assembled to the body. This included all glass, wiring harnesses, lights, the instrument panel gage cluster, convertible top and/or hardtop, radio, door locks, hood latches and support, headlamp doors and motor, steering column, brake and clutch pedals, etc. The 1963 coupe back lights (windows) were held in place with a rubber gasket like earlier model car windshields were mounted. This assembly leaked water as the FRP dimensions were not stable enough to guarantee a good fit. The 1964 and later coupe body back light was held in place with an adhesive/sealer much like current automobile windshields are assembled today. Several variations of adhesive were tried. One adhesive/sealer was kept frozen in a deep freeze until applied and cured as it came to room temperature. Another was cured when it came in contact with water, accommodated by the water test. The material used in later years was more stable as it is today. The many different adhesives were used in an effort to improve the process, reliability and quality.

---

2 *Corvette Paint Finishing System* by R. H. Grosbeck, February 25, 1963 Detroit Section, Society of Plastic Engineers, Reinforced Plastic Group

CHASSIS LINE

The Body Shop, Paint Shop and Trim Shop conveyors all went around corners, usually in a serpentine shape. The Chassis Line was straight. The frame was placed on the line upside down where the differential and front and rear suspension were attached. The frame was rolled over using a chain sling to pick up the partially assembled chassis and manually rolling it over.

The brake master cylinder was installed on a support bracket or fixture and the brakes were bled. The remainder of the drive line including the dressed engine/transmission assembly was then installed. When the electrical, air conditioning, fuel system, ignition, fan, etc. were assembled to an engine we called it "engine dress". Then the exhaust is "buttoned up", slang for completed, to the engine, the fuel tank and lines were then assembled, etc. The various chassis components were then lubricated and the chassis made ready for body drop. Front wheel bearings were lubricated and the retaining castle nut and cotter pin was assembled. The hub cap was set on the front tire by the production worker. The inspector checked the cotter pin installation and assembled the hub cap. This is the only assembly operation I know of that was performed by an inspector.

BODY DROP STATION OR "MARRIAGE"

Body Drop was labeled "Marriage" by assemblers as it is the mating of the body to the chassis. The Trim Line ended about midway in the Chassis Line. The body was picked off the body truck with a special over head hoist that picked up the body under the wheel openings. The hoist was moved manually on a short conveyor to the body drop station where it was lowered onto the chassis that had been previously checked and shimmed on the chassis line to match the body. Missing or improper shimming will affect door fits and place unnecessary stress on the body. Long drift pins were used to guide the body onto the mounts.

Operators in a pit under the line final assembled body bolts and the connection of various electrical and mechanical components.

A few gallons of gasoline was added to the fuel tank, pre-mixed water and antifreeze in the radiator and the engine was ready to start for the first time. Before connecting the radiator hose to the engine, a stick of stop leak, the operators called it a "dog turd", was placed in the thermostat housing. Starting was generally not a problem. However, fuel was slow getting to the fuel pump prolonging cranking time and stress on a new battery. This was expedited by installing a special cap on the gas tank and inflating the fuel tank with 5 to 7 psi (pounds per square inch) air pressure to push fuel to the fuel pump. Once started the special cap was removed and a proper one installed.

ROLL TEST STATION

Roll Test was performed at the end of the Chassis Line. The station consisted of driving the "job" onto rollers about 18 inches in diameter, two under each rear wheel with an air actuated lift pad between them to assist in getting the job on and off the rollers. There was one roller under each front wheel, driven by the rear rollers. The rollers were smooth on one half and about 2 inches out of round on the other half. The operator sat on a makeshift stool as there were no seats or carpets in the job at this point. The operator who started the engine at the end of the chassis line, drove the job onto the Roll Test Station. He then reached out the window, pressed a button on a post that lowered the job 2 or 3 inches in the rear onto the rollers. Simultaneously, rollers raised out of the floor in front of the rear wheels to prevent the job from getting off the rollers during test.

This test only checked drive line function, brake function, speedo calibration (correct gear ~ about 40 mph), front and rear light functions etc. The job could be steered side to side as the front wheels were rolling also. The operator/driver could steer from the smooth portion to the out of round portion of the rollers and test for rattles. Rattles could not be easily heard over the roller noise and side mounted exhaust on some jobs. Upon completion of the Roll Test, the operator/driver pushed the button again raising the pad between the rear wheel rollers and lowering the restraint rollers allowing the job to be driven off.

Immediately following the roll test, the job was driven onto the front wheel toe-in machine that set front wheel toe in with the wheels rolling. Front wheel caster and camber and rear wheel camber and toe-in was set on the chassis line during assembly.

WATER TEST

Following Roll Test, every job was driven into a water test booth where a deluge of water from specially located water nozzles drenched the job. The driver started the water test with the headlights and it stopped after 4 minutes, minimum.[3] Water leaks were documented and repaired. A retest was performed to verify leak repair.

The most common water leaks were windshield, back light and the plenum area.

HEAVY REPAIR

Following Water Test all major defects were repaired. Such things as non-functional electrical circuits, removal and replacement of defective transmissions, engines, brakes, water leaks, etc. were repaired. In fact, anything that was wrong at this point of assembly was fixed off line in Heavy Repair.

PAINT REPAIR

Heavy Repair was followed by Paint Repair. During Trim installation, Body Drop, Roll Test, Water Test and Heavy Repair chips and scratches could occur to the paint job. Paint defects such as sags, dirt, porosity, orange peel etc. were also corrected in Paint Repair. The Paint Repair system was designed to

---

3 *1963 Corvette Assembly Manual, Section 14, Sheet A6.00, Water & Vacuum Water Test.*

handle 225% of production. That means every job went to paint repair twice and one in four went three times. Some went more than three times. We wanted the best possible paint job.

Sometime around 1965 it was decided that the paint repair system in use was not completely adequate. A "spoven" was purchased for about $50,000 I was told. The spoven was a spray booth that included an electric oven for curing the paint. This improved paint quality and repair time significantly.

Bond joints were almost impossible to hide with paint. Knowing where the joints are makes them fairly easy to detect. The bond material was prone to blister or form small holes from porosity. We did our best but I think every Corvette shipped in those years had a visible bond joint some place on the body.

FINAL LINE

The Final Line was a straight line also. The first station was paint polish. Two men, one on each side, full time, polished the entire job with rubbing compound and polishing wheels. John Turek, of Chevrolet Central Office in Detroit, who later became my boss, said the new Corvettes on the Final Line looked just like Easter Eggs they shined so much. This is where all the top brass like Semen E. 'Bunkie' Knudsen, Elliott M. "Pete" Estes and other V.P.'s viewed the jobs.

They all liked coming to ST. Louis to see the Corvettes.

Following polish, the convertible lid edge trim, carpets, door trim panels, seats, plenum grilles, windshield wipers, radio antenna trim/adjustment, door sills, seat belts, jack and wheel cover stowage, etc. were added. Corvette radios needed an adjustment, called trim adjustment, in those years to match the radio to the antenna for optimum performance.

The last operation was headlamp aim and headlamp bezel installation. Then the shining new complete Corvette got its window sticker and a coat of shipping wax. They left the plant looking very drab, but under that wax was a thing of beauty, a fresh 1963 or '64 or '65 or '66 or '67 Corvette Stingray Convertible or Aero Coupe on its way to an eager customer.

CHAPTER 3

✦ ✦ ✦

DOWSMITH INC.
ASSEMBLY PLANT

DowSmith Inc. - Ionia, Michigan

Corvette assembly in St. Louis was a popular place for Chevrolet executives. Howard H. Kehrl, Manager, Chevrolet Central Office Quality Control Department, Later Chief Engineer, Oldsmobile Division, visited, as did Augie Slatinsky, Supervisor, Procedures & Audit, Manufacturing Assembly, John Turek, Body and Frame Group, and many others from many departments within Chevrolet including Product Engineering, Industrial Engineering and many others. I came to know these men through the Outgoing Quality Audit, Especially Augie Slatinsky and John Turek.

November of 1963, I was approached by John Turek, Supervisor of the Body and Frame Group, Chevrolet Central Office in Detroit. John asked if I would be interested in a position in Detroit. During that same time frame, I was approached by Augie Slatinsky, Supervisor, Procedures & Audit, Manufacturing Assembly, with a similar offer. I said yes to both supervisors. I traveled to Detroit soon after for an interview with John and Augie. I was met at the airport by Gerald "Jerry" Vogelei, Administrative Assistant to Ed Gray, Director of Quality, Chevrolet Division. Jerry and I were close friends until his death in 1995.

I interviewed with Augie Slatinsky first and we had lunch together. His opening was one of auditing the quality of finished cars in all of Chevrolet's 14 assembly plants nationwide, a continuation of my work in St. Louis. I interviewed with John that afternoon and learned that his opening dealt with the coordination of quality with the Mitchell-Bentley Body Company, later DowSmith, in Ionia Michigan and Chevrolet St. Louis.

Before John finished telling me the content of the job, I said "I know who I want to work for". John quickly said, "Wait, not too fast, I am not finished yet." I said, "That is okay, I want to work for you." I will never forget the look on his face. He was grateful and I grew to honestly love the guy, one of my best bosses.

Being wanted is grand.

My assignment was to perform liaison between Chevrolet St. Louis and the Mitchell-Bentley Body Company in Ionia, Michigan to coordinate the quality of bodies to be built in Ionia with those built in St. Louis.

My first visit to the Mitchell-Bentley Body Company was Wednesday, December 4, 1963. When I arrived, I was greeted by George MacFarlane, Chief Engineer and many of his department. I liked George and began a long term friendship with him and many of his staff, including his right hand man, Don Mirzoian. Don Deeb was another engineer that I came to know and appreciate. The plant was old but well organized and clean. Look at the floor in Image 1 at the end of this chapter.

I was told that the building began as a furniture factory as Michigan was home to many furniture companies. It was a large facility of two five story buildings tied together with a tunnel or closed bridge on the upper floors. The buildings had wood floors supported by wood columns and used high cycle electric devices for most on line operator use, unlike most assembly plants that use compressed air for hand tools. I was surprised how the operators used a paddle shaped tool with exposed copper wires shaped like hooks that they hung over bare exposed wires about eight feet off the floor to connect their electric tools. The paddle shaped connection slid up and down the wires making movement very easy. I learned that the power source provided 400 cycle at 24 volts so it would not shock the operators. I was impressed.

The Mitchell-Bentley Body Company produced Limousine bodies for Chrysler in the 50's and Buick and Oldsmobile "C" body (full size) station wagon bodies for the 1958 through 1964 model years until General Motors ended production of those models. Full size cars were designated as "C" bodies and the next smaller were "A" bodies. During those years, almost all GM car bodies were built by Fisher Body Division. Bodies built by Fisher Body exhibited a name plate on the door sill incorporating their logo, a stage coach with the inscription "Body by Fisher". The station wagons built in Ionia by Mitchell-Bentley exhibited a logo on the sill plate stating "Body by Mitchell-Bentley, Ionia, Michigan".

When the contract for station wagon bodies ended, General Motors awarded production of the Corvette body to Mitchell-Bentley. Rumor had it that there was a close relationship between Don Mitchell and a top executive of GM. It was suggested that GM felt obligated to Mitchell to not allow the company to close. So, GM awarded the Mitchell-Bentley Body Company a contract to produce half of the Corvette bodies for Chevrolet St. Louis. What ever the reason for awarding Mitchell-Bentley the contract, second shift production of Corvette bodies ceased or was diminished at Chevrolet in St. Louis. There was no space problem associated with the suspended second shift. This move was taken as a near insult to the St. Louis Assembly Team. The initial reaction in St. Louis was that the Corvette body could not be satisfactorily built by anyone but the St. Louis Team and they set out to prove that point.

Chevrolet policy for dealing with outside supplier quality issues was by issuing a Defective Material Notice (DMN) for the reporting of parts that did not meet specifications. The DMN was also used to charge a supplier for rework or replacement of defective parts. The Chevrolet Central Office Quality Control Department administered the DMN process with the assistance of Chevrolet Purchasing. Eddie Lamb was the negotiator for Chevrolet Central Office Quality Control. Eddie was very effective in his work. His approach was simple. Chevrolet had 14 assembly plants in those days and many suppliers serviced several or all of the plants. When Eddie got a DMN from one plant and the supplier resisted back charges, Eddie simply asked the supplier, "Maybe I should ask some of our other plants if they are having a similar problem with your part". The supplier usually accepted the back charge without further argument. Eddie was great.

Shipment of finished bodies from Ionia was an initial concern. We were not sure how much handling the body could tolerate without material damage. So, we ran several tests before settling on rail. The Inspection Department in St. Louis had a Portage Double Quick (PDQ) surface plate and measuring system of a size capable of measuring a complete body. The PDQ system was like a height gage that could reach every point on the body. We placed a coupe body on a special checking platform that looked a lot like a build truck. My friend and co-worker, Monty Brawley, was an expert on the PDQ. He scribed, as marking with deep scratches, lines in the body at critical elevations and longitudinal points and we documented the points of intersection. Our boss remarked, "You guys are producing junk". Monty and I just looked at each other and proceeded. The objective was to see if the body changed while in transit between St. Louis and Ionia. We then bolted the body to a steel shipping skid that did not have the dimensional characteristics or rigidity of a body truck or the Corvette chassis. The body was shipped by rail on a somewhat vertical 'A' frame then again in car position like finished cars are shipped. A g-meter devise was attached to the rail car to see if there were any unusual vibrations experienced in-route. We were suspicious of rail practices in Chicago as we had reports of excessive 'rail car humping' in the Chicago yards. Humping is when a rail car is released at speed over a distance to expedite moves and stopped when it hits adjoining cars or a dead end. No significant changes in body dimensions was observed.

The Ionia Mitchell-Bentley Body Company had been building car bodies for many companies for over 30 years including General Motors for many years. They had an engineering department capable of designing car bodies for production and for show. Ionia had years more experience building car bodies than St. Louis. They immediately processed the body, examining released parts against requirements, reporting errors to Chevrolet Engineering for correction. Prior to the Mitchell-Bentley work, the accuracy of released parts in the Bill of Material was not significantly important as only one assembly plant was producing the body. When a second plant began producing the same body, the Bill of Material needed to be accurate. The Mitchell-Bentley Body Company was more qualified to build the Corvette Body than was Chevrolet. However, the Chevrolet St. Louis Corvette Team did not agree and I did not try to change their mind.

When the Ionia produced Corvette bodies began to arrive in St. Louis, the St. Louis Team judged them harshly. A DMN was written for each body with a long list of defective parts to support the back charges to cover the repairs. The St. Louis Team was treating DowSmith with unmerciful cruelty in my opinion. The back charges for quality repairs were excessive. Removed parts were returned to Ionia in 4' X 4' X 4' skid boxes like rocks with little explanation other than statements like "Did not fit" or "Defective" or "Damaged", etc. The St. Louis Team was taking their animosity out on the Ionia Team when the Ionia Team was not entirely at fault. I was hard pressed to explain the actions of the St. Louis Team to the DowSmith people.

Soon after the contract was awarded to Mitchell-Bentley, the business was sold to A. O. Smith and the company was known by that name. Then, in 1965 Dow Chemical bought a share of the business as there was an interest to build a fiberglass reinforced plastics plant and the company became known as DowSmith, Inc.

Mr. R. Indreica was the Quality Manager when I first visited the Ionia plant. He retired in April 1964 and was replaced by Mr. R. Hanson who came from A O. Smith in Milwaukee, Wisconsin. Mr. S. M. Englund of Dow Chemical in Midland, Michigan replaced Mr. R. Hanson in July of 1964. This was about the time that Dow Chemical of Midland Michigan became a part owner of A. O. Smith Ionia and the name changed to DowSmith Inc. Then in December of 1964, Mr. John Wygent replaced Mr. S. M. Englund for the balance of the contract thru the 1967 model.

The rapid turnover of Quality Managers by individuals who, I believe, did not have automotive assembly plant experience contributed to inconsistencies in the body quality. The Outgoing Quality Audit of finished bodies reported demerits or issues that ranged from a low of 10 demerits per body to a high of 100 demerits per body.

Initially, the quality of the Ionia body was not as good as that of the St. Louis body. Back charges may have been justifiable. My job as liaison Quality Engineer was difficult. I personally inspected bodies in Ionia with an effort to match the St. Louis standard. The Ionia team resisted my input but realized that I represented Chevrolet and exerted great effort to satisfy my inspections. I wrote a Memorandum to my boss, John Turek, weekly following my visit to Ionia and St. Louis on alternate weeks.

I wrote a letter to John Turek, my supervisor, dated June 15, 1965 with copies to Jim Steen, Assistant Manager Allied and Outside Sources, John's boss, Charley M. Bodwell Manager Quality Assurance, second in Command to Mr. Ed Gray, Director of Quality, Chevrolet Division and Don Babcock, Chevrolet Central Office Purchasing reporting the turn over in the Quality Manager position. The following summarizes that memo.

January 1964 - The first 5 bodies shipped in January, 1964 were shipped with known defects. When the quality manager, R. Indreica, was confronted, he said, "Ship the bodies and let's see how St. Louis receives them."

February 1964 - 100% inspection by Chevrolet drove total demerits per body down to about 10 per body.

March 1964 - Defective Material Notice (DMN) back charges dropped from $51.20 per job at start up to $4.36 and Chevrolet Audit inspection was withdrawn.

April 1964 - Quality deteriorated and back charges went to $5.00 per job and average demerits were about 100 per job.

May 1964 - Chevrolet 100% Audit inspection resumed.

June 1964 - Demerits per body were down to about 30 and back charges were at $2.89.

February 1965 - Demerits per body had risen to 70 per job.

June 1965 - Bi-weekly Chevrolet Audit inspection decreased demerits to about 35 per job.

The first line of the last paragraph of that June 15, 1965 memo to John Turek, states: "The Dow Smith Audit does not assist the plant in improving quality." The management did not use the Outgoing Quality Audit as a tool to feed issues back into the assembly process for corrective action.

My June 15 letter was forwarded to DowSmith top management by Don Babcock, Chevrolet Purchasing where it circulated to the top of the DowSmith organization who sent it back to Chevrolet top management with side bar notes. Eventually, it came back down the chain of command to John Turek, my supervisor, who informed me, "You have become a very popular writer" as he showed me the circulated memo. John said to me, "don't worry, you are not in trouble". I was relieved.

The Corvette body was difficult to assemble as there was a lot of work that depended upon operator finesse and ability. The St. Louis Team had the edge here. They had several years of hand crafting experience over Ionia. The Ionia approach was a little different. For example, the headlamp door openings were over filled with bond material and then sanded to fit the die cast headlamp doors. This was performed by hand in St. Louis. Ionia built a sanding fixture or tool that prepared the openings much like a machining operation resulting in a more uniform and consistent opening.

Door fits were a problem for both plants. Doors were built oversize to the door opening and the gap between the door and the door opening sanded to acceptable appearance. St. Louis had developed a method whereby two sanding discs were mounted on a disk sander back to back and inserted in the door to body gap thus simultaneously sanding the door and the opening at the same time to achieve a somewhat consistent gap.

Hood fits were a constant problem for both plants. The hood and front fender upper panels were supplied to both plants by the Molded Fiberglass (MFG) Body Co. in Ashtabula, Ohio. Hoods were prone to be over crowned, that is high in the middle along the sides. St. Louis corrected this by splitting and re-bonding the Front Fender Upper Panel to Wheel House Inner Panel bond joint along the side of the hood opening and raising the Front Fender Upper Panel to match the hood. This was frequently performed after finish paint and after Body Drop. I detested the practice but had no alternative for the practice except to work with the supplier. We began 100% inspection of hoods in St. Louis and Ionia and returned many racks of hoods to Ashtabula. Both plants became suspicious that the other plant's rejected hoods were being shipped to the other plant. So, Ionia stamped each rejected hood on the underside near a corner with a small ink stamp. Some of those stamped hoods were found in St. Louis and returned to MFG. So, the Molded Fiberglass Body Company watched for the stamp and sanded them off. Then the racks of hoods, all with the same sanded area in an area where sanding was uncommon and very obvious, were observed in the other plant. This cat and mouse game went on for a while and eventually hood quality was brought under control. We had high suspicions that the rejected hoods went to service.

Eventually, the St. Louis Team grew to accept the Ionia bodies, but not with open arms.

April 1965, DowSmith Inc. held a "Molding Plant Dedication and Open House". Fiberglass plastic trays measuring 11" by 17" were molded as gratuities for visitors. I still have a few that we use daily. Images 1 through 8 that follow are from the hand out that was created for the opening.

The DowSmith Plant in Ionia is gone, it was raised August 1995. I visited the site recently and was saddened that the rail siding is gone and there is no trace of there ever being a factory where Corvettes were once built.

DowSmith Inc.
production specialists in both
reinforced plastic
and steel automotive bodies
and components

Image 1

complete engineering service

planning   We can do our best for you when we "get in early" — to assist you on initial planning. Whether the product is to be reinforced plastic or steel, if it's right on paper, it's going to be right when it goes into production.

design   DowSmith maintains a complete staff of experienced engineers who perform product design functions as well as design and engineering services on interior and exterior trim, body structure and finishing including methods and materials. By this means we provide the best possible product at lowest possible cost.

prototype   A complete prototype service is available to you. Before a body or component starts down a production line, it has been thoroughly "pre-tested" in our Experimental Engineering Laboratory. Every phase of manufacturing is completely examined so that quality meets or exceeds customer requirements . . . costs remain within customer budgets.

production   DowSmith production facilities include efficient production lines from complete automobile bodies and component assemblies to modern fabricating facilities for individual components. Materials might be reinforced plastic or steel — or can be as varied as you choose to make them. In the case of plastics, facilities include molding, fabricating and finishing of products or components, in small runs or quantity production.

resources   DowSmith comes by its unique abilities naturally. Extraordinary research talents and laboratory facilities possessed by the Dow Chemical Company assure the best in resin and chemistry technology. From A. O. Smith comes a tremendous background in mass-production techniques, design, metals fabrication and welding know-how. Result: a high degree of production excellence which is transmitted to the customer at each stage of design, development and manufacturing.

Image 2

fabrication . . . reinforced thermosetting plastic

DowSmith is equipped to mold almost any component or complete product that can be designed of reinforced plastic. DowSmith facilities include every standard molding method — to be of complete service regardless of quantity requirements. (See Below) Presses ranging in size from 72 to 1600 tons for matched die molding use either mat, preform or premix methods. We are also equipped with a wide range of preform machines — 48″ to 156″.

1. matched metal die molding — preform and mat — This method can mold parts at production rates to precise dimensions. Major advantage of this technique is its high-speed production possibilities with low-cost tooling. The parts have uniformly high strength and physical properties, and a consistently good surface finish requiring minimum finishing. Advanced manufacturing equipment enables us to meet your high quality standards. **2. matched metal die molding — premix** — In such a system the reinforcing materials, resin and fillers are combined in a doughy mass that is placed in metal molds and quickly cured by heat and pressure. Advantages include fast production rates, high quality surface finish and design possibilities that permit complex parts with inserts, ribs and molded holes, etc. Low cost and a broad variation of physical and chemical properties are other plus features. **3. open mold — sprayup** — Benefits of this technique are fast production rates and low-cost molds — an ideal method where large parts are required. This method uses the same type of molds used in hand layup, but the reinforcing material and plastic are applied with spray guns. **4. open mold — hand layup** — Prototypes, panels, containers, housings and ducting are popular applications for this technique. Advantages of this system are low-cost molds, lack of size restriction, and the ability to produce parts with little lead time. Wood, plaster or reinforced plastic molds are utilized.

A special customer-benefit is our careful concern with **process control.** Such activity — backed up by continuous chemical laboratory quality control of resins and glass—result in uniform high quality of reproduced parts. This means more production in less time; directly benefiting customers with lower costs. Research facilities at DowSmith's Little Rock plant, The Dow Chemical Company and A. O. Smith Corp. are also called upon to satisfy your needs.

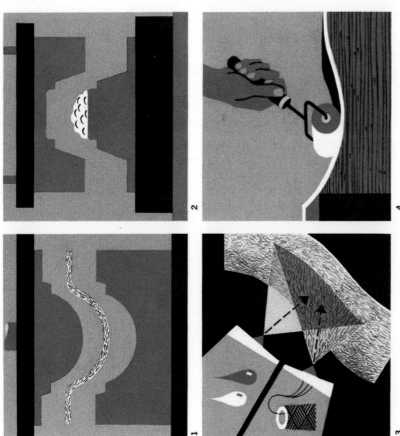

Image 3

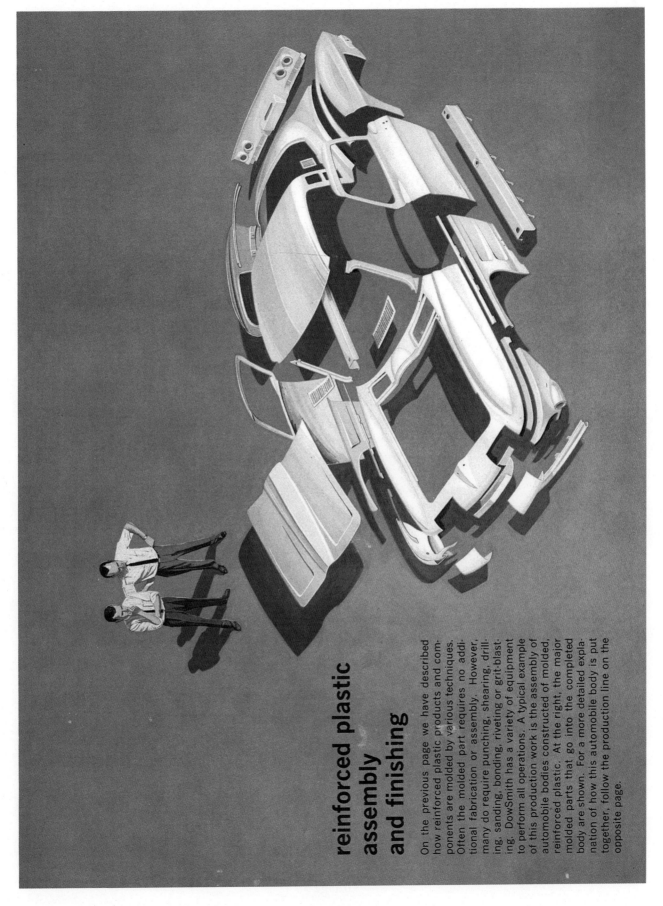

reinforced plastic assembly and finishing

On the previous page we have described how reinforced plastic products and components are molded by various techniques. Often the molded part requires no additional fabrication or assembly. However, many do require punching, shearing, drilling, sanding, bonding, riveting or grit-blasting. DowSmith has a variety of equipment to perform all operations. A typical example of this production work is the assembly of automobile bodies constructed of molded, reinforced plastic. At the right, the major molded parts that go into the completed body are shown. For a more detailed explanation of how this automobile body is put together, follow the production line on the opposite page.

Image 4

1. **off and running** Early stages of moving conveyor assembly line with various mounting brackets being fitted to underbody, while "birdcage" is being assembled to underbody structure. Subsequent stages of structural and component assembly are seen in background. **2. off the beaten track** Detailed components with supporting reinforcements are bonded together into sub-assemblies. Assembly of other components such as doors and fenders is also performed off-line. **3. sky's the limit** The convertible body is nearing the end of DowSmith's assembly line. Portions of convertible top mechanism are installed at the same time as other final plastic components are bonded in place. **4. rubdown** Drysanding excess bond preserves the sharp styling feature of the body; also maintains smooth surface at joints that otherwise would require trim molding. Here, too, doors are fitted and hood and body assembly is completed.

2.

3.

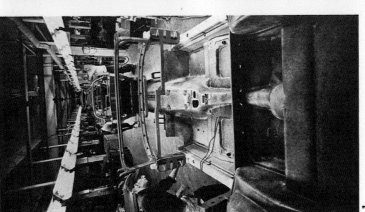

1.

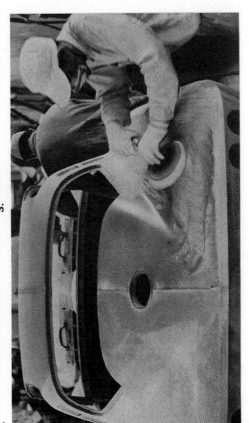

4.

Image 5

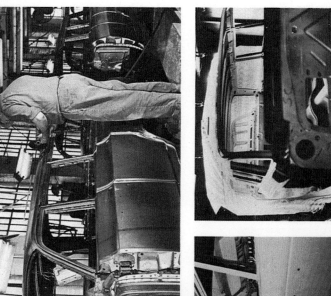

steel body assembly and finishing

DowSmith steel assembly capabilities are best demonstrated by our production of station wagon bodies. Indeed, for more than a decade the Ionia plant has been the largest independent producer of this specialized variety of automotive body. From the beginning of the assembly line until the final check-out before shipment, the secret of our success has been constant control of all production techniques. Body assembly, trimming and finishing are done with painstaking care to insure that the final product reflects our good name . . . but more important the good name of our customer.

1. here welding is a science Electric welding equipment in the hands of skilled operators transform components into a complete station wagon body in this main jig where major welding operations are performed. **2. each body goes to finishing school** As the bodies move along the metal finishing lines, sanding, polishing and other finishing operations are performed. Each operation is checked and double-checked to eliminate any flaw on the body's surface. **3. rainbow booth** Central mixing room dispenses paint through 6 miles of piping to guarantee the application of consistently true colors. Whatever the color nothing is left to chance in obtaining the most breathtaking showroom effect. Both manual and electrostatic spray methods are employed. **4. the heat's on and under control** In this high-temperature infra-red oven, the finish on a station wagon body is baked to perfection. Bodies move through the baking ovens from the paint booths in a carefully-controlled stream.

Image 6

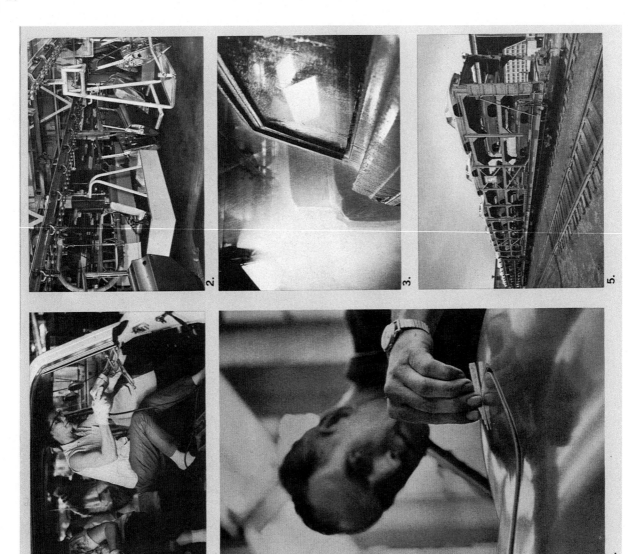

final assembly — both reinforced plastic and steel

Whether the body is reinforced plastic or steel, it requires final testing and inspection before it is shipped to its ultimate destination — anywhere in the world.

1. trimming for action At this point on the line, these station wagon bodies are nearly complete. As the bodies move along, pre-assembled interior trim is installed. **2. coordination** Installation of seats assembled at DowSmith takes place on final assembly line. Seats move in on a separate conveyor system, synchronized so that the right color combination and options arrive just at the moment when the body for which it is intended reaches the proper point. **3. taking a bath** This station wagon body proves its water tightness by getting a much stiffer shower than it would receive in any commercial auto wash. **4. final quality audit** Checking the finished product for mechanical and visual characteristics and assigning outgoing Quality Rating are functions of DowSmith's Quality Auditor before the auto body continues on its journey to the outside world. **5. special delivery** Our plant — situated in the heart of the automotive industry — is ideally located to serve the great industrial empire of the Midwest. Two railroads as well as the interstate road system serve Ionia.

Image 7

who is DowSmith?

DowSmith is a company formed and jointly owned by two highly respected names in American industry — The Dow Chemical Company and A. O. Smith Corporation. The Ionia Division specializes in the assembly of steel or reinforced plastic automobile bodies and in the production of reinforced plastic automotive components. Another division, located at Little Rock, Arkansas, manufactures pipe, fittings and other high-strength products of glass fiber reinforced epoxy.

DowSmith Inc.
IONIA DIVISION
IONIA, MICHIGAN

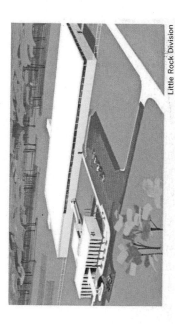

Little Rock Division

Assembly, Ionia Division

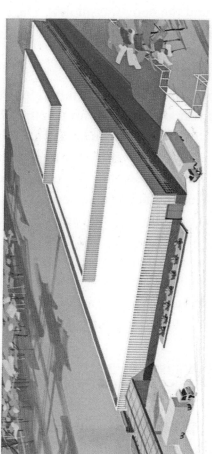

Fabrication, Ionia Division

nearly a million square feet of production space

The Ionia Division of DowSmith Inc., located in Ionia, Michigan, is centered in two separate but adjacent facilities. Assembly facilities are located in a complex of buildings totalling nearly a million square feet of production space and containing modern, efficient assembly equipment. A newly constructed plant with 80,000 square feet of space contains molding equipment, and provides for production methods and process controls that are far advanced over anything in the molding industry.

DSI-501 3M 8-64

LITHO IN U.S.A.

Image 8

CHAPTER 4

+ ◆ +

DESIGN CHARACTERISTICS
AND BUILD PROBLEMS

LAUNCH

Corvette Launch of the 1963 model was a major undertaking. The chassis was almost completely new and different and the body was all new. The body really was different than anything built before. The fiberglass reinforced plastic (FRP) panels were bonded to bonding strips riveted to a metal frame dubbed a "bird cage".

The first 1963 Corvettes built in St. Louis were mixed in with the last of the 1962 model. Corvette production of the 1963 model year and running through the 1967 build were produced at a rate of six per hour. The first 1963 Corvette built in St. Louis was put on line in early August while still running 1962's. Parts to support this individual unit were placed along the assembly line at the proper locations so that production workers could learn the assembly process unique to the 1963 Corvette. After evaluation of the initial pilot job, a second job was built the same way. Less than ten jobs were built this way, most going to international and local car shows. I doubt any were sold.

I was inspecting a coupe and reported that the water temperature, oil pressure, ammeter and fuel gages did not work. I was informed that these gages and instrument panels were hand made at a cost estimated to be $50,000 each, including tooling, and would be scrapped and replaced with production parts when available. This was my introduction to the cost of building cars.

These jobs were examined and re-examined by almost everyone in the St. Louis Assembly Plant and by a host of people from Detroit Central Office. People from Detroit collected data from us, the St. Louis plant employees, and reported back to Detroit as if it was their own, usually not giving credit to the source of the information. We began to catch on and referred our Central Office visitors to other sources. We coined a name for the Detroit visitors, COSOB's. (Central Office SOB's). We had a lot of laughs at the expense of some of the COSOB's. I later became a COSOB.

I was a new employee at the time of the launch so was more of an observer than a contributor. I was standing in a group of manufacturing, quality and engineering men, there were no women in the plant at that time, observing the birdcage build. The initial assembly of the birdcage was troublesome. Production was learning, engineering was justifying their designs and quality was "pointing fingers" at everyone. Quality people were labeled "Finger Pointers" who were accused of having one finger pointing at the problem and three pointing back at themselves.

This Birdcage build meeting was becoming heated. I was standing by Howard Kehrl, Manager, Chevrolet Quality and later Chief Engineer, Oldsmobile Division, who said to me "Here's how you do this Larry, you wait until everyone states his position and then you summarize the highlights back to the group.". After a few minutes Howard stepped into the front of the meeting and summarized the positions of others into a single statement. Everyone got quiet, listened and after a brief discussion, Howard's comments became the basis for the solution required to solve the problems. I never forgot Howard and tried to use his method whenever I could in my career.

The 1963 Corvette build was very labor intensive. Every assembly station in the Body Shop required creative craftsmanship. Every part that became part of the body required some amount of assembler "fitting" to work. A metal part might need a little extra bend or a plastic (FRP) part might need a little special trimming. Worker skill was critical.

Every part of a current automobile is interchangeable. That is, all doors of a particular model car will fit on every car of that model. Not true with the 1963 thru 1967 Corvette. Doors were unique. Headlamp doors were unique in the beginning, later die cast doors were more interchangeable. Every body was sanded, not too much to expose fiberglass strands and not so little that the surface was not smooth. Bond joints were worked and reworked to make them invisible under the paint.

The Aero Coupe was a challenge from beginning to end. The coupe door Upper Inner Reinforcement Panel has a small bracket with a small oblong hole about 1/4" by 3/8" that is used to secure the door window outer Seal Assembly. The area where this small bracket is attached to the Door Upper Inner Reinforcement Panel has a tight radius shape that is visible just above the Door Trim Panel after assembly. This area of the door Upper Inner Reinforcement Panel is not to drawing contributing to the poor fit that results in a hole between the door trim panel and the door. This was visible from prototype parts and was never conquered.

I am not sure if any customers complained but the designer did not like the result. When the part was released for quote, no stamping company quoted the part because the tool to produce the part could not be built. To form the part, the tools would be 'die locked'. That is, the tool might shut, come together, but would not open after forming the part.

Purchasing informed the Budd Company, who 'no quoted' the job, that if they wanted to supply Chevrolet full size car front fenders, hundreds of thousands per year, they would product the 1963 Corvette Aero Coupe Door Upper Inner Reinforcement Panels. Budd got the job and did a good, not perfect, but close. The parts are in every coupe built.

By some standards, Corvette Launch may have run on through the 1964 model year. There were so many new processes introduced that it seemed like a constant 'new process' launch. Such things as the introduction of fixed glass, like windshield and back window seals, were replaced with a rubbery bonding material. Introduction of four piston brake calipers that were difficult to bleed of air bubbles. Engine ignition shielding to prevent spark noise on the radio.

When center mount wheel and tire assemblies were introduced, torque of the large three 'ear' retaining nut was at issue. Questions like how much torque is required? How do we assure proper torque? How do we audit the torque? The assembly manual instructed operators to strike the retaining nut 'ear' with a special lead hammer two times. What was the resulting torque? Were they tight enough? Would they come off in service? Most operators hit them three or more times to 'make sure'.

The Inspection Department was very concerned. A torque wrench with capacity to 1,000 Foot Pound capacity was purchased with a special adapter constructed to attach the torque wrench to the retaining three ear nut. The first attempt to use the wrench was comical. The wheel retaining nut on the left side of the job has right hand threads and those on the right side have left hand threads to favor tightening under operation rather than loosening. When we attached the six foot long torque wrench to the front wheels with the handle extending forward, we pushed down on the long wrench and got a reading of about 600 foot pounds to loosen the nut as engineering prescribed. With the wrench extending rearward on the rear wheels to clear the body we needed to pull up on the wrench. The combination of the applied wrench torque and lifting up on the job caused the wheel to slip or spin on the floor before reaching the torque value required to loosen the nut. All had a big laugh. The wrench would need to be placed on the nut along side of the job so we could push down on the wrench to load the wheel so it would not slip. This was not possible with our adapter because the body interfered with the wrench. A new adapter was made and more torque values were recorded. Many retaining nuts were marked to detect movement under driving conditions. After much discussion and testing it became apparent that two blows to the retaining nut ears was adequate and reliable.

CARPETS

The 1963 Corvette floor carpets were cut from flat material and edge bound. Since all of the pieces were flat, each flat piece was installed separately over jute pad. The various pieces were frequently cut from different dye lots which posed a constant color match problem, especially with red.

Beginning in 1964, the floor carpets were one piece moulded to fit the under body contours. This reduced the number of pieces considerably and reduced installation time and variation. The pad under the carpet also functioned as a sound deadener. The pad was made of an unwoven cotton scrim about 1/4" thick adhered to a rubber like backing about 3/32" thick.

The pads were installed with the cotton scrim next to the under body and the rubber backing on top or next to the carpet. The design intent was that road noise would be dampened in the cotton scrim and reflected off the rubber backing where the sound would dissipate or die in the cotton scrim.

EMBLEM LOCATING

The FRP panels were received without holes for nose, body side and rear emblem mountings, removable hard top deck mounting hardware, etc. Following the first dry sanding of the body and before any paint, the mounting holes were drilled. Their location was established using a drill basket fabricated of fiberglass, metal and plaster. The drill basket was made by taking an impression from the master body to fit the body contour. The drill basket was made so the operator could locate it on the body contour with tabs to reference the edge of an opening like the door or hood opening. Drill bushings were mounted in the drill basket to precisely locate the holes with repeatable results.

FIBERGLASS REINFORCED PLASTIC (FRP)

All of the FRP panels, that is, all bonding strips, hood and door inner and outer panels, roof, underbody, fenders, etc., used in the 1963 through 1967 Corvette body were made in matched metal dies. That is, the parts were pressed between two metal dies, one shaped like the inside of the panel and the other shaped like the outside. The matched metal dies formed the panels at a constant .100 inch thickness. The die half that formed the painted surface or concave side of a part was the female half and the die half that formed the inside or convex side of the part was known as the male half. The dies were steam heated to cure the fiberglass.

The process for making an FRP part became an art to provide a good surface finish for painting without resin rich or poor areas.

Resin rich areas occurred when the glass reinforcement material separated or tore upon die closing. Since the glass strands tore or broke, these areas were not reinforced resulting in a weak area that cracked. Resin poor areas occurred when the resin did not completely fill the gap between the die halves leaving the glass strands exposed. The result was a very porous and weak area that could not be painted. These areas almost always occurred in radius areas such as the front fender upper panel in the corners of the hood opening, headlamp door opening, plenum grille openings, etc. The front fender lower rear panel, behind the front wheels, suffered this problem around the louvers.

Manufacturing of an FRP part began by spraying chopped glass strands coated with a binder onto a screen shaped and contoured like the part. A vacuum behind the screen pulled the chopped glass in place during the short cure cycle. This glass mat was then placed over the male half of the die which was usually the bottom. Next, resin was hand poured over the mat in a pre-measured volume in a specific pattern to control resin rich and resin poor areas. The measure was often a prescribed number of one pound coffee cans of resin. I believe volume of resin was only critical to cost. Then a layer or sheet of very fine strands of fiberglass like the angel hair used around the base of a christmas tree was placed over the mat and the poured resin to help hold down the ends of the chopped glass to improve surface finish. The matched metal die was then closed pressing the FRP to shape and uniform thickness. The die remained closed for several minutes while the part cured.

Following the moulding process, the part was trimmed, repaired as necessary and spot sanded.

CONVERTIBLE TOP

The 1963 Model Convertible Top was supplied by Findlay Industries in Findlay Ohio. Phil Gardner started the company in his garage with three employees in 1958. By 1963, Findlay Industries had grown to a large company supplying interior trim to many manufacturers including the manufacturer of Piper Cub aircraft. I knew Phil personally and respected his efforts to provide a superior quality convertible top for the 1963 Corvette for the production run through 1967.

The convertible top was called a baby buggy top because it was attached to the body like a baby buggy top, that is, all in one piece. Conventional convertible tops of the day were tacked to the body along the rear. The corvette top was attached to an extruded aluminum rear bow which incorporated a large rubber seal. This bow and seal assembly was designed to fit snugly to the convertible top deck lid. None of the tops sealed to the deck lid and many owners complained about water coming forward on the deck lid when driving in heavy rain. Car bodies, especially those that are not completely tight like the Corvette, experience a negative pressure inside when under way. This adversely affects water leaks and adds to the above problem. Water ran up hill from the convertible rear bow seal towards the driver falling into the luggage well behind the seats. Owners complained.

This problem was addressed late in the build, around 1966 or 1967. Product engineering was reluctant to change the seal design because they believed the parts were not to drawing. My supervisor, John Turek, assigned me the responsibility of confirming that the rear convertible top bow was to drawing. I traveled to the part supplier, Ashtabula Bow and Socket Co., in Ashtabula, Ohio to confirm the quality of the rear bow as they had the only checking fixture. I inspected many parts and confirmed that the parts were in fact to drawing. A meeting with Product Engineering and General Management, including the V.P. of Chevrolet Manufacturing took place soon after at the GM Tech Center in Warren, Michigan.

There are three 'notches' in the rear bow locking pin. Sealing was designed to be complete in the second notch or mid point of vertical travel between the convertible top rear bow and the deck lid. Sealing was not complete even when in the third notch or full travel of the latch. This was demonstrated by my supervisor, John Turek. The V.P. of Manufacturing said, "I sure would like to see how that looks without the Seal". John grabbed the seal and pulled it off the rear bow as it is not glued. The seal slides into the extruded rear bow like a key. The rear bow was returned to the latch design position and the gap between the body and the bow was constant. The seal was simply too small to seal the top to the rear deck.

Engineering admitted they had a problem and a new, larger section seal was released. This change improved the sealing but the problem was never completely eliminated.

SEATS

The 1963 Model Seats were also supplied by Findlay Industries in Findlay Ohio.

The seat tracks in early Corvettes had a propensity for sticking and jerky movement. I was working with the seat manufacturer, Findlay Industries, who was building the seat to design as closely as possible. The seat track, produced by McInerney Spring and Wire Co., was just not robust enough to work well.

The seat track design engineer was a young engineer as were all of us. He designed a seat track so strong that it would work fine under any condition. The prototype passed design validation testing with flying colors. The design called for four mounting feet or tabs that bolted to the underbody. The mounting area of each tab was specified to be on a plane with each other within a tolerance of plus or minus .010 inches.

The supplier said that to achieve that degree of accuracy, the frame would require machining at a premium. We held a meeting with Product Engineering and any change in the seat at this point meant re-running the validation testing at a estimated cost of $25,000. The design engineer, who was in budget and on time at this point, saw his performance rating waning.

I said "The seat frame is so strong that the underbody of the Corvette will yield to the strength of the seat frame and still work fine. So why not open the tolerance from plus or minus .010" to plus of minus 1/16" and the seat will still work fine and we won't need to machine the mounting tabs?" Eventually all agreed, the change produced a workable seat and everyone was happy.

Corvette bodies supplied by DowSmith included completely trimmed seats using the same parts that the St. Louis Team used. Both plants received the seat frames, seat foam pads and seat covers separately. Both plants assembled the seats.

LEATHER SEAT TRIM

We were having trouble producing satisfactory leather seats. Some of the seats looked sub standard like wrinkly "belly" leather. Semen E. "Bunkie" Knudsen, Executive Vice President, Chevrolet Div., was scheduled to tour various assembly plants and of course Corvette, St. Louis was on the list. When a VP makes the rounds, anybody that is anybody is there. My ultimate boss, Ed Gray, Director of Quality for Chevrolet Division was there. Mr. Gray asked me to go with him to support him if Mr. Knudsen asked any questions that he might need my assistance. I was honored.

The tour group came to the Corvette plant where I joined Mr. Gray. Everything was going well until we hit the Corvette final line where the seats were installed. Mr. Knudsen was big on quality and when he saw the leather seat option he asked, "How much is the leather seat option?" Someone said, "About $80.00". Bunkie said, "You mean to tell me that we are charging customers $80.00 for leather that looks like this?" Some apologies flew around and finally Mr. Knudsen said, "We are not shipping any more Corvettes with this kind of seat trim, Stop the option." The leather option was stopped until we got better seats.

Since I was the Supplier Quality Engineer assigned to seats, it became my job to work on improvement. We asked purchasing to call in some suppliers of leather for automotive seating. Several came to the meeting bringing leather samples with them. We talked about the problem and solutions for a while and told the suppliers that we would get back to them after we examined the samples.

My boss, John Turek, and I looked at the samples together and decided that we alone could not set the standard. So, John, my boss, in his infinite wisdom, asked Charlie Bodwell, Manager, Quality Assurance of Chevrolet Central Office to take a look at the leather with us. Charlie did not like making fast decisions and usually deflected them. John asked Charlie what he thought of a particular sample and Charlie said it didn't look too good. The next sample he asked Charlie the same question and Charlie said it was better. John picked up the pace and Charlie was answering right along. John was piling the samples that Charlie liked in one stack and the ones he did not like in another stack. Suddenly, Charlie exclaimed, "Hey, you are making me sort the samples". John smiled broadly and said, "Yeah, and you are doing a good job". We all smiled on the outside and laughed on the inside as Charlie excused himself. That sort was a good start and we soon had what we thought was an acceptable range of leather quality.

The suppliers were appraised and one responded, "You are going to have better leather seats in the Corvette than Cadillac." John said, "That's what we want" and that is what we got. Then we began to discuss who had the authority to turn the option on again. After all, the VP turned it off so he or his representative should turn it back on. After some deliberation, we recommended reinstating the option to Ed Gray, Director of Chevrolet Central Office Quality that we were confident that the leather seats were satisfactory. The option was reinstated.

A few weeks later I was in the St. Louis Corvette plant and Lou Biskach, Chevrolet St. Louis Plant Manager, came up to me on the assembly line floor and put his arm around me and said, among other things, "Hell Larry, we can't tell a cow how to grow its skin, can we?"

VINYL SEAT TRIM

My efforts to acquire the best quality seats was progressing well. Then, Chevrolet Purchasing informed me that Brad Osgood of Textile Trim in Detroit had issued a quote for production of "Black Only" seat trim covers and ask that I survey their facility to determine their capability. I contacted Mr. Osgood and met him at his factory on 12 th Street in Detroit on August 13, 1964.

The facility looked capable but the process equipment was not as good as Findlay Industries. I wrote and submitted my report thinking I had pretty much filled my obligation. I was told that Brad had quoted complete black trim covers at a price lower than Findlay Industries could buy the materials. This was alarming to the Chevrolet Purchasing and Quality Departments. The Purchasing Agent, Don Babcock, was cautiously optimistic and asked that I continue working with Textile Trim.

Sample trim covers were submitted and I inspected them along with Central Office Sample Inspection people who worked for Mike Meyers. Everything looked satisfactory with the dimensional inspection so we issued an approval pending laboratory inspection/testing of the materials. Lab. failed.

I was not surprised or disappointed. However, Brad at Textile Trim wanted to know what test failed so corrective action could be pursued. The lab. report simply said, "Failed Cold Crack". I became very involved with investigating Chevrolet Labs. to determine just how the test was run. I got very evasive answers from the Lab people. They would not tell me how the test was performed saying that the test was proprietary. Well, I worked for Chevrolet and refused to accept that answer. After many phone calls up the organization ladder, I was granted a visit to the Lab.

Cold crack testing of vinyl at that time was performed by stretching a sample of the vinyl over a two pound coffee can and securing it with a rubber band. The can and vinyl was placed in a deep freeze for a soak period (24 or 48 hour at 0 or lower degrees). Following the soak, the test specified that a 5 pound steel ball of 2" diameter was to be dropped from 4 feet onto the vinyl. I did some quick math and asked the technician where he found a 2" diameter ball that weighed 5 pounds. He blushed and said that the ball was 2" diameter and might not weigh 5 pounds. A 2" diameter steel ball weighs about one and a quarter pounds. After dropping the ball on the vinyl, the vinyl was rolled over a 1/4" diameter rod to look for cracks. Cracks produced by either method was cause for rejection.

I informed the Textile Trim vinyl material supplier how the test was conducted but left out the coffee can part. I said it was a 6" cylinder. After a period of time, vinyl was supplied that passed the cold crack test and some trim covers were produced by Textile Trim. I did my job but was not happy.

AERO COUPE DOORS

The aero coupe roof panel did not fit the bird cage in the beginning of the 1963 model build. The problem showed up as a gap between the roof panel and the top of the lock pillar on the very first jobs built. The gap was as much as a 1/2 inch wide on both sides. This Joint is in the contour at the rear of the door opening where the roof comes down and then sweeps out to the fender peak line. This joint was filled on very early bodies but was deemed objectionable by plant management.

Correction of this problem was achieved by lowering the bird cage roof line about 1/2 inch. The roof panel to lock pillar gap was closed but many more problems developed. When the roof panel was laid over the bird cage, the 1/2 inch gap appeared at the top of the lock pillars because the roof panel wrapped around the bird cage and was too small to reach the lock pillars. Production decided that a 1/2 inch bond joint at the top of the lock pillars was unsightly and likely not reliable. So, the bird cage was lowered 1/2 inch to reduce the lock pillar to roof panel bond joint to a more desirable thickness. Both Chevrolet St. Louis and DowSmith Ionia received the seat frames, seat cushions, seat covers, etc. separately. Seats were assembled in both plants. DowSmith attached the seats to the body with two bolts for shipping. St. Louis removed the seats upon receipt and stored them for later use.

Now the doors extended above the roof panel about 1/2 inch.

Correction of this problem was achieved by bending the top of the door down and then inward to match the roof height. This caused the door to be outboard of the body so the top of the door was edge ground to allow the door top to move inboard to help the contour of the door to match the body contour. This "bending" exercise was accomplished by a strong operator who placed his knee at the rear of the door at the bottom of the window DLO (Day Light Opening) and manually pulling the top of the door inboard. The DLO is defined by the window opening through which light will pass, usually smaller than the glass size. A kink is evident in many1963 thru 1967 aero coupe doors as shown in Image 9.

Image 9

Additionally, the contour at the top of the door does not blend properly with the roof panel, as shown in Images 10 and 11. The roof sweeps gently downward from the center of the body to the door opening and then the door top tends to look flat in respect to the continuation of the roof sweep.

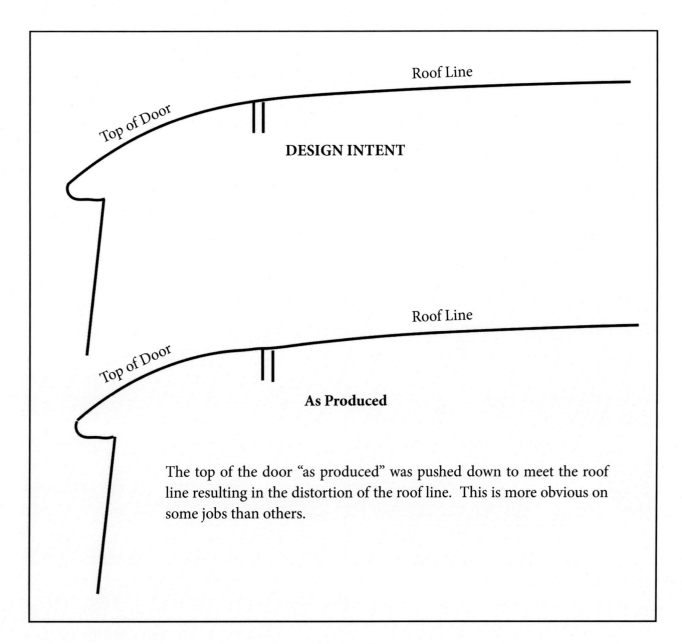

Image 10

This is the result of bending the door down at the top. This departure from styling is more prevalent on some bodies than others but can be seen on many aero coupes. The result was a door that fit better but a window assembly that was, in some cases, not functional. The effort to raise the window the last inch or so was very high. Electric windows would not close in some cases. The bending of the door caused the glass sash to move outboard at the bottom resulting in interference with the door glass lower weather strip. The weatherstrip was ground to form a ramp and lubricated to allow the sash to slide by the weather strip. This rework, shown in Image 12, allowed the windows to close but now the glass digs into the glass channel fuzz strip near the bottom of its travel as shown in Image 13.

Image 11

Some doors were made to fit with a less severe process that resulted in a fit that looked like the door is not fully closed as shown in Image 14[4].

This was how many of the doors were finally built and delivered.

The bending and grinding of Aero Coupe doors to make them fit really bothered me. I asked Ed Teskie, Superintendent of Production on Corvette, for permission to build a coupe that was as close to design as we could get it. He said Okay. We had two Bird Cage assembly fixtures and really only used one, the other was backup. The Bird Cage checking fixture was certified upon delivery. I then began adjusting the backup weld fixture to create a bird cage that would satisfy the requirements of the checking fixture. After 8 or 10 birdcages were produced in the back up fixture, I got a bird cage that fit

---

4 Photo by Richard DeMay of Farmington, Michigan.

the checking fixture very well. All of the bird cages that I built were used as they were all closer to design than those that we were building.

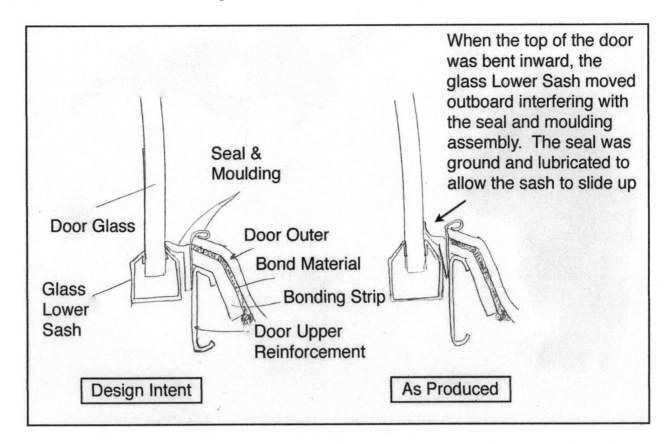

When the top of the door was bent inward, the glass Lower Sash moved outboard interfering with the seal and moulding assembly. The seal was ground and lubricated to allow the sash to slide up

Seal & Moulding

Door Glass

Door Outer

Bond Material

Bonding Strip

Glass Lower Sash

Door Upper Reinforcement

Design Intent

As Produced

Image 12

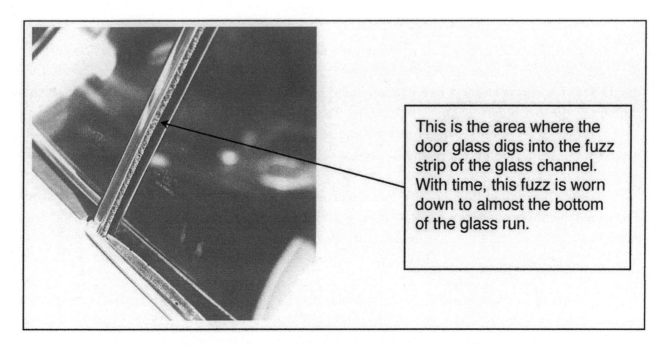

This is the area where the door glass digs into the fuzz strip of the glass channel. With time, this fuzz is worn down to almost the bottom of the glass run.

Image 13

Image 14

I followed the build of the Corvette that used my "special" bird cage and the doors fit perfectly. However, we had to "butter up" the joint between the top of the lock pillar and the outer panel. I was thanked for my efforts and was told that we would continue to bend and grind the doors rather than "butter up" the lock pillars.

I was disappointed but learned an important lesson. The job of Quality Control and Inspection people is to investigate and report conditions that degrade quality and it is managements job to decide what to do about it.

Sometime during the 1965 or 1966 build after two or three years working on the problem it was discovered that the roof panel was not to drawing. Why we did not check the roof die to drawing, I will never know, probably no time. The doors were repeatedly checked and found to be to drawing by use of a "Splash" off the master body. Doors were always at least 1/2 inch too tall to the roof.

The roof panel die was made to the wrong side of material. The roof was too small. The surface of the male die half that formed the inside of the roof should have been the size of the surface of the female half that formed the outside of the panel. The result was that the roof was .100 inches undersize. The tolerance stacking effect of the parts resulted in the 1/2" gap over the lock pillars.

Correction of this problem would have required a complete new aero coupe roof panel die when the body was about to go out of production. By the time the problem became known, the roof panel die had been chrome plated to improve the surface finish of the roof panel. A new die and chrome plating costs were considered but not purchased because of the short time remaining in the build.

DRIVE LINE VIBRATION

Sometime during the 1964 or 1965 build, a drive line vibration became apparent. Drive shaft balance was checked and rechecked and none found out of specification. Differential yoke balance was checked and no problem found. A fix was attempted for the more severe cases. Radiator hose clamps were attached to one or both ends of the drive shaft to provide a balance weight. If the vibration got worse the clamp was rotated 90 or 180 degrees on a trial basis until the drive line vibrations were considered acceptable. Some number of jobs were shipped this way.

While this activity was going on, other investigations were under way. Drive shafts are marked at the rear yoke for high balance point and the differential yoke is marked for the low balance point. These marks are to be matched as nearly as possible at assembly. There are only two positions. Observation of the assembly line showed that the marks were properly aligned sometimes and not at other times. The assembler was questioned and it was learned that this person had not been on the job long. When asked about aligning the marks on the parts, his reply was "What marks?" Needless to say, the problem was corrected immediately.

If the drive line in your Corvette vibrates, try rotating the drive shaft relative to the differential yoke 180 degrees.

SPARE TIRE MIXUP

The 1963 Corvette had 15 inch wheels. Sometime in 1966 or so, the Corvette plant ran out of 15" wheels. To keep production running, it was decided to get a supply of 14" wheel and tire assemblies from the passenger plant to keep production running until 15 inch assemblies could be supplied. All Corvette leaving the plant were quarantined waiting for replacement wheels.

No 14" spare tires were to be installed in the spare tire carrier.

The 15" wheel and tire assemblies were received a few days later and all quarantined Corvette were canvased and corrected. Problem resolved.

Some time later, and it was not that long, a customer complained that he had a 14" spare tire and others complained that they had no spare tire. This underscores the fact that 100% inspection is only about 85% effective.

CHAPTER 5

✦ ✦ ✦

LABOR RELATIONS

LABOR

Chevrolet St. Louis was my introduction to manufacturing labor and specifically the UAW. Initially, I did not have direct interface with the UAW worker so I was very much an observer. I was hired as a Quality Analyst whose work did not directly involve the hourly worker. However, a few months into my work, I was required to attend 'Foreman Training' classes. This turned out, in my opinion, to be training on how to get along with the UAW employee. I enjoyed the training and soon came to really appreciate it. The training focused on the relationship between union and management. The training defined what I should expect from the union employee and what he should expect from me. The relationship between labor and management was not adversarial but I thought guarded, for a lack of a better word.

The management of labor within an assembly plant is a major task that would be difficult without the union organization. The union leadership provides assistance to the Plant Management staff through the enforcement of Shop Rules[5] and the Contract Agreement. When the union makes its demands public, as it does with work stoppage, etc., the union appears adversarial.

Without the union, management would be required to deal with each employees issues separately. The "Agreement" between the union and management includes a four step Grievance Procedure clearly stating how employee issues are to be addresses.

Step One - Presentation of Grievance to Forman. This step is usually a one on one discussion between the worker and his foreman. Note that political corrections was not an issue in 1961 so all employees were addressed as "his" and his supervisor was a "foreman" on the shop floor. When I worked as a foreman over 30 or 40 hourly employees later in my career, I kept a little note pad in my pocket that

---

5 Employees' Handbook of Rules and Regulations that included Time and Pay Regulations, Safety and First Aid, General Regulations, Shop Rules and 41 General Safety Rules and Regulations. Violation of any of the rules and regulations could result in disciplinary action ranging from reprimand to discharge.

I recorded discussions with my workers including date and general issue. Some issues were raised by the worker and some by me. The workers under my supervision knew that I only documented the issue for future reference to support the next step of discipline if it became necessary. Most step one resolutions were concluded with verbal warning or sometimes a written verbal warning that was not issued to the committeeman. I never had an issue go to step two.

Step Two - Appeal to Shop Committee. Plants with a large number, hundreds, of employees had committees and sub-committees by department to provide focus on the kind of work being performed. The step 2 issue became a formal grievance that was documented and forwarded to the committeeman for his use to present the issue to the shop committee. The shop committee consisted of several members who attempted to resolve the issue. When the shop committee could not resolve the issue the grievance went to step three.

Step Three - Appeal to Corporation and International Union. This step is much more involved and takes on the appearance of a civil court. When this action does not resolve the issue, step four follows.

Step Four - Appeal to an Impartial Umpire. Appeal to an impartial umpire can be requested by the Union or by the Corporation. This step further extends the resolution of the issue.

Issues or grievances between the union and the corporation were collected and used as bargaining chips at the time of contractual agreement ratification.[6]

There were 11 pages of *Wage Rates* listing 41 Utilityman classifications and rates, 26 Reliefman classifications and rates and 123 *Job Classification* rates attached to the Chevrolet St. Louis Agreement. A worker who was classified as a 'Assembler, Cars, Cabs and Commercial Bodies' received $2.65 per hour, hiring rate and $2.75 per hour after 90 days on the job. The highest paid Job Classification was for skilled trades workers classified as 'Electrician Leader' and 'Pipe Fitter Leader' at $3.46.

Minutes of the Local Demand Meeting between Chevrolet St. Louis Management and the Local Union Representatives dated September 19, 1961was also attached to the "Agreement".[7] This meeting was attended by 7 Chevrolet St. Louis management representatives and 12 union representatives. The minutes consisted of 21 pages of 70 demands of which 47 were 'Withdrawn without prejudice.' The remaining 23 were concluded with mutual agreement between the management and union representatives. This committee, on this date, also adopted 18 items published in *Local Shift Preference Agreement* attached to the "Agreement".

The Union at the Chevrolet St. Louis plant was designated Local No. 25. Additionally, there were 5 pages devoted to the Local Shift Preference Agreement, 1 page to a local Memorandum of Understanding, 13 pages of Wage Rates specific to St. Louis and 15 pages of Local Seniority Agreement information.

---

6 The *Agreement between General Motors Corporation and the UAW-AFL-CIO* dated September 20, 1961 consisted of 152 pages in a 4 by 7 inch booklet.

7 *Minutes of the Local Demand Meetings* dated September 19, 1961 containing 70 Local Demands

All of the above were provided in a 4 by 7 inch booklet. The point here is to provide an understanding of the massive undertaking to manage the work force under such voluminous requirements.

I formed my opinion of Union Workers from no knowledge of their practices. Some events that did influence my opinion of the union were hard for me to accept. We had some turn over in employment that did affect quality. There was a line worker who, being paid at the end of the week, habitually missed work on Mondays. He was asked why he missed so many Mondays, working only 4 days a week. His reply, "I can't make it on 3 days". I do not think he made it to the 90 day contractual requirement that would have afforded him a $0.10 per hour raise and for a secure position.

One morning as I entered the plant, I saw a lot of hubbub going on in Heavy Repair. I walked down to the area and saw a Corvette Coupe lying on it's roof between two hoists. Repairmen changed transmissions by placing a post (pipe) under the engine and lowered the hoist slightly so the cross member supporting the transmission could be removed allowing the transmission to be removed. I was told that the job was left on a hoist with the pipe in place by the second shift repairman and the hoist leaked down pushing the job off of the hoist. We all wondered how much noise was made and if the late night janitors were alarmed. The job was removed from the area and not much was said afterwards. I believe the chassis was salvaged and some other undamaged parts. The body was scrapped.

There were a number of Corvettes built for celebrities and for factory delivery. The Shriner Masons from Kansas City ordered about 18 Sebring Silver convertibles with red interiors for their parade unit. Some had no heaters or radios, some had not vinyl top but a hard top, some even had not top at all. The Shrine Masons showed up in their Fez and white outfits to drive back to Kansas City in convoy. Hardtops were shipped separately so they all left the plant with tops down, if they had one, in a very colorful convoy. They were a great bunch of guys that hung around the plane most of the day before leaving.

When there was an order for a celebrity, the celebrity's name was written on the windshield. One was built for Doris Day so her name was on the windshield when it came off the line. There were quite a few jobs built with celebrity names on the windshield. The name on the windshield practice was stopped because there seemed to be more defects on jobs with a celebrity name displayed. It was suspected the jobs were sabotaged because of the name. There was no proof.

One day the stars of the TV series *Route 66* appeared in the plant. Image 15 shows the actors with a 1960 Corvette. The series was popular at the time and I watched it often. George Maharis who played Buz Murdock and Martin Milner who played Tod Stiles hung around the plant for the better part of a week. I met them and enjoyed their company. They drove a Saddle Corvette Coupe back to the studio when they left. I was impressed and enjoyed their visit.

Corvettes and Route 66

The TV series debuted in 1960 by CBS Adventure Series. Filming 116 episodes and starring Martin Milner, George Maharis and Glen Corbett, this is one of literally hundreds of motion pictures featuring Route 66 as its backdrop.

Image 15

The assembly workers did not always get along well together. An incident developed as a result of an inspector who was beaten after his shift, more than once. Investigation of the matter revealed that the perpetrator of the beating worked on the line ahead of the inspector. When the inspector documented the workers defective work, the workers foreman disciplined him for faulty workmanship. So, the assembler took his frustration out on the inspector. The inspector was a good worker but became very cautious about documenting defects and he got in trouble for that. Many of the workers entered the assembly process without much understanding of relationships such as exist between an assembler and an inspector.

I was walking the Final Line one day and observed the assembler who installed the drivers seat. There was a small nick in the leather seat cover and the installer was applying red paint to hide the nick. I asked him what he was doing and he said that he was repairing the seat. I asked him if he would be happy with a new Corvette with a touched up seat. He said, "Yeah, no big deal, it won't show". I continued my walk down the line and when I got to the end I looked back down the line. The assembler was removing the seat. I went back and complemented him on his decision and he just smiled and said "I wouldn't want a repaired seat". Most assembly workers had a good work ethic and were proud of their work.

A more disappointing event took place one night in the summer of 1963. I came to work one morning and observed a hubbub in heavy repair again. There was a convertible Corvette in heavy repair covered with a tarp. I looked under the tarp and found a totally destroyed Corvette with blood and other evidence of a horrific accident. Finished O.K. Corvettes were driven from the plant to a marshaling yard for storage awaiting shipment to dealers. The distance was about a quarter mile and the gate to the yard was only wide enough for one job. Drivers drove the jobs to the yard and were ferried back to the plant as more jobs were completed. It was learned that some drivers liked to race to see who could get to the gate first. The wrecked Corvette was the result of a driver who lost the race and his life in the process.

Occasionally jobs were loaded onto Complete Auto Transit (CAT) trucks at the back of the assembly plant. One afternoon there was a loud crash just outside of the plant. Some of us ran out to see what happened and found a Corvette Coupe upside down in front of a CAT truck. It seems that the truck driver who loaded the job on the platform over the truck tractor cab failed to secure the park brake and after climbing down, the job rolled off the front of the truck onto the ground. Corvettes do not fair well with such treatment. It was not uncommon to salvage parts from damaged jobs. I spoke out about the practice but was over ruled in most cases.

Many things happen in an automobile assembly plant that seem to be without control. That is why they are called accidents. However, some practices were not accidents and are not allowed today. Management of the Corvette Assembly Plant were allowed to drive O.K. Corvettes home over night. There were six or eight such employees that enjoyed this privilege. The preparation for this practice involved adding enough fuel, in addition to the standard 3 gallon fill, to allow the job to be driven the distance of perhaps 50 miles. The speedometer was disconnected and a slave speedometer was installed so the driver could monitor his speed. The odometer mileage out and in was recorded on the inspection ticket to document total miles driven. The purpose of this practice was to assist in the evaluation of the product for quality purposes. No one questioned the practice. Executives from Chevrolet Central Office in Detroit were sometimes afforded the same courtesy when they were in St. Louis on business.

The Chevrolet St. Louis Corvette Assembly Plant workers were respectful men. My dad, Richard A. Galloway, visited me at the Corvette Plant a time or two. Dad was a natty dresser, sometimes told by others and admitted himself that he was a clothes horse. One Fall day in 1962 he came to the Corvette Plant dressed as usual; suit and tie, black top coat, grey leather gloves and a Homburg hat. Dad always looked sharp. He was once accused of looking like Harry Carey, the legendary Sports announcer for the St. Louis Cardinals. Dad was waiting for me outside the guard house where many of the employees entered and exited the plant. It was shift change time and as the workmen passed by Dad on their way out of the plant, many opened their lunch box and showed the empty contents to Dad. Dad politely observed the lunch boxes and said nothing as he did not understand what was going on. He related this event to me later when we met that evening. Dad asked me why the workmen showed him their empty lunch box. I explained to Dad that the workers were cautious and being polite. They did not know if Dad was a part of plant or company security or just a visitor. So, rather than tale any chances, they politely displayed their empty lunch box to show that they were not taking anything from the plant that was not theirs. Dad was amused but respectful of the workers.

My 15 month initiation to the auto industry in St. Louis was a highlight of my career in Quality. I learned much and developed a lasting standard of practice that I carried with me through my 45 year work history. I met many great people who I will never forget.

CHAPTER 6

✦ ✦ ✦

MY PERSONAL CORVETTE EXPERIENCE

When I was in the 7th grade, someone ask, "What do you want to do when you grow up?" I quickly replied, "I want to work for General Motors." That came true August 16, 1962 at Chevrolet St. Louis. I was of the opinion at that time that General Motors was the best car company in the world and it was unquestionably the largest. There was Ford, Chrysler, Packard, Studebaker, Hudson and Nash but General Motors and especially Oldsmobile was my favorite. I began to repair cars as soon as I got my drivers license. I was fascinated by the mechanical workings of cars and preferred auto mechanics over most things. I replaced the engine in my 1952 Oldsmobile with an engine from a 1956 Olds. I was told by the head mechanic of our local Olds dealer that it could not be done. After completing the swap, I drove it to the dealership to show my work to the head mechanic and he refused to look at my car or to acknowledge that I had done it saying, "It's impossible". That swap is another story but is an example of my enthusiasm for automobiles.

After high school, I completed my education in Mathematics at Western Illinois University. I worked for the Electric Wheel Division of the Firestone Tire and Rubber Company as a draftsman. Then I took a position as a Mathematics Teacher in a small high school during which time I received a "Greeting" letter from Uncle Sam. I was deferred for the balance of the year. I enlisted in the Army Reserve before my teaching assignment ended and became active the following June 1960. After the Army, I taught Mathematics again in a Junior High School.

In the Fall of 1961 my desire to work in the automotive industry returned. I had no idea how to apply for a position with General Motors so I wrote a letter to General Motors, Flint, Michigan. I no longer have a copy of the letter I wrote or what I got back. I did receive a letter from GM advising me to contact my local dealer and pursue employment through the dealership zone office. I went to my local Chevrolet Dealer and was advised to contact Mr. Leon C. Dorn, Zone Manager in Peoria, Illinois, my home state. I was surprised and excited about receiving a response just five days after I sent my letter. I wrote Mr. Dorn a number of times and every response was less than a week. He advised me to contact Chevrolet St. Louis, the plant that supplied cars to our local dealer. I wrote a letter to the personnel department in the Chevrolet St. Louis Assembly Plant and in a short time I received a letter from H. C. Von Arx, Supervisor Salaried Personnel Administration, Chevrolet St. Louis. After a few more letters, I received the letter shown in Image 16.

The letter invited me to visit Chevrolet St. Louis on June 20, 1962 at 9:00 AM. June 20, 1962 was an exciting day for me. I felt like a privileged character. I met with Mr. Von Arx and others including Ken Brooks, Chief Inspector, Jake Bass, Assistant Chief Inspector and several others. I was conducted around the Chevrolet St. Louis Assembly Plant including passenger car assembly and truck assembly. I have always enjoyed building things and watching and learning how things are built.

CHEVROLET - ST. LOUIS

DIVISION OF GENERAL MOTORS CORPORATION

3809 UNION BOULEVARD

ST. LOUIS 15. MISSOURI

June 14, 1962

Mr. Larry M. Galloway
2063 Vermont Street
Quincy, Illinois

Dear Mr. Galloway:

Thank you for your letter of June 11, 1962 advising us of your
continued interest in Chevrolet-St. Louis and your desire to
visit the plant at an early date. With respect to the dates you
indicated which would be convenient for your visit, it would
appear that Wednesday, June 20, 1962 would be a most satisfactory
date from out point of view. I would suggest that you plan to
arrive at the plant at approximately 9:00 a.m. on that date so
that we will have ample opportunity to become familiar with our
operation.

If anything develops which should make this date inconvenient,
I would appreciate your early advice. Otherwise, I will look
forward to seeing you on June 20.

Very truly yours,

H. C. Von Arx, Supervisor
Salaried Personnel Administration

HCV:ma

Image 16

I was returned to Mr. Von Arx's office and we chatted for a few minutes. He asked me when I could start if I were to be offered a position. I told him that I had a vacation planned with my family the first two weeks of July and could begin immediately after that. He told me to contact him after my vacation and we could discuss the opportunity again at that time. The family vacation was in Florida so St. louis was on the way home from our vacation.

We stopped in St. Louis in mid July and I visited Mr. Von Arx again. Again he asked me when I could begin employment if a position was offered. I said, "Now". He said that he could not extend an offer that day but advised me to begin looking for housing. He said that I could expect a letter of employment with the start date and pay rate soon. I was ecstatic. I went home in anticipation of a letter of employment. It was mid July and I had not signed my teaching contract in anticipation of employment with Chevrolet. The mail came on Monday, July 30, 1962 and no letter arrived. I watched with great anticipation every day after that. When no letter arrived on Friday August 3, I became very worried. I called Mr. Von Arx that afternoon and told him that I was anxiously awaiting his letter. That I had a teaching contract to sign on or before the 10 th if there was no opportunity for me at Chevrolet. He said, "I am so glad you called, we have been extremely busy and I have not had time to prepare a letter for you. Your start date with Chevrolet St. Louis will be Thursday, August 16, 1962 if you wish to accept the position." I said, "That is fine. What time should I report?" He said. "We start work at 7:00 AM but any time before 8:00 AM that day will be fine. A letter of employment will be forthcoming."

I could not believe it. I got the job. I believe to this day that I would not have gotten the job if I had not called on that Friday, August 3.

I was there before 7:00 AM, Thursday, August 16, 1962. A day I will never forget.

I began work on a Thursday, August 16, the first day of a pay period, because we were paid on the 15 th and the end of each month or 24 pays a year. I met with my boss that first day, Mr. Ken Brooks, Chief Inspector. I liked him from the moment I met him. He said, "We have a new department that we are starting, it's called 'Quality Control'. Would you like to be part of that?" I was not sure what that was but I was so enthused that I responded with a firm yes. He said that I would work with Don Lovshe for a while to learn about Quality Control.

Don told me that our focus in Quality Control was on an audit of the quality of finished cars and trucks, known as the Outgoing Quality Audit. We used a check sheet of about 5 pages so the inspection of every car covered the same items. After a couple of weeks inspecting full size Chevrolet cars and trucks, I was told to begin the audit of Corvettes in the building just west of the main plant where Corvettes were assembled.

When I arrived in the Corvette plant the assembly lines were filled with 1963 model Corvettes. Bob Blubaugh, Inspection General Forman of Corvette took me on a tour of the lines. As we walked down the Chassis Line there were a lot of convertibles with the top up, rear bow up, doors open with the door glass up. I closed the door of one of the convertibles and the door glass cut to convertible cloth top. Bob said, "That's okay, we can put a new top on that one". I felt bad. Then on the very next job, I did it again. Bob said, "that's okay, we can put a new top on that one too". Now I really felt bad. Obviously, I never forgot that incident.

Corvette production was set at six per hour so each work station was 10 minutes. A lot of work can be accomplished in 10 minutes. Each operator had a lot of parts to assemble making the line shorter by comparison with higher production rates. Passenger car assembly in the main plant, for example, was 60 per hour so each operator assembled his parts in one minute making the number of parts involved much less.

Initial production of 1963 Corvette was chaotic. The repair area was choked with jobs. Every kind of repair imaginable was addressed. Everything from paint repair, water leaks, engine changes, transmission changes, hood fits, and much more were addressed. Repairmen worked overtime so many hours they were found sleeping under the jobs. After a few weeks of this, Lou Biskach, Chevrolet St. Louis Plant Manager, announced the end of overtime. He said, "If we cannot repair what we build in 8 hours we will build what we can repair in 8 hours. We will immediately begin assembly for 4 hours and repair for 4 hours until we get production under control". Repair overtime stopped and we achieved 8 hours of production with no overtime for repairs in short order.

OUTGOING QUALITY AUDIT OF FINISHED CORVETTE

My assignment was to conduct an Outgoing Quality Audit of finished Corvettes. Five jobs were selected at random from final inspection accepted production each day and were inspected by a union inspector that I worked with and supervised in the audit process. I reported to Marty Voss, Corvette Inspection Forman, who was the union inspector's supervisor. I collected the audit data, compiled it and held an audit review with plant inspection and production supervisors each day. A typical report is shown in Image 17.

The numbers in the parenthesis refer to the frequency of defects followed by the demerits assigned. We used the term 'defect' freely for some time. That was before the legal department became involved and informed us that Chevrolet did not manufacture defective cars, they may have problems, but not defects. Later we were advised that problems must be changed to issues. Chevrolet cars and trucks are not produced with defects or problems, but may have issues. I will continue here with the verbiage as we spoke it.

Defects that could affect safety were assigned 20 demerits. Safety items included such things as defects associated with the brakes of braking systems, door latch defects, headlamp door operation, etc. Defects that resulted in a problem that a customer would go immediately to his dealer for repair were assigned 10 demerits. This included functional items like windows that would not go up or down, inoperative deck or hood latches, etc. Defects that a customer would likely tolerate but have repaired at his next visit to his dealer were assigned 4 demerits. Defects such as poor fit of components, sizable paint defects, etc. Defects that could cause customer dissatisfaction but not likely to cause the customer to seek repair were assigned 1 demerit. Such things as small paint chips, scratches, miner emblem fits, etc. The report in Image 17 shows the average demerits per job (car) at 41.5 for the month of March 1963. That report is for a 1963 Aero Coupe Serial Number 111770 that came off the assembly line on March 29, 1963. The SOURCE DEFECTS are defects attributable to components purchased from outside suppliers.

CORVETTE AUDIT
SERIAL NO. 111770

MODEL 837   DATE PRODUCED 3-28-63
INSPECTION
SHIFT RESP.   AVERAGE DEMERITS PER UNIT FOR MONTH OF MARCH 41.5

	DEFECTS INSIDE	DEMERITS
1	1. Interior paint scratched in two (2) places	2

DEFECTS OUTSIDE

2	1. L. fender emblem doesn't fit	1
2	2. Exterior paint chipped in three (3) places and and scratched once.	4

DEFECTS UNDER HOOD

1	1. Windshield washer hose routed through hood release	4

DEFECTS UNDER BODY

1	1. Front end alignment:	Camber L & R 50' Total toe 5/32" in	2
	2. Passenger inboard seat belt bolt misses rubber cushion		1

SOURCE DEFECTS

1. R C/V doesn't seal at bottom	4
2. L & R windlace caps cut lock pillar cover	2
3. L & R windshield post garnish not down against seal	2
4. One (1) body crack	1

PAINT DEFECTS

1. Interior:	Off color (1)	1
	Dirt (1)	1
2. Exterior:	Surface pits (1)	1
	Poor repair (1)	1
	Over grind (1)	1
	Dirt (3)	3
	Clean up (1)	1

WATER TEST:	Light leak at L & R C/V	2

TOTAL DEMERITS	34

Image 17

WATER LEAKS

I was assigned the task or reducing Corvette water leaks in July of 1963. The water test was conducted after roll test at the end of the chassis line and before final trim where all interior trim, including door trim, carpets and seats were installed.

There were two water test booths, one static and one vacuum. The static booth was equipped with many water nozzles that sprayed water on specific areas of the job, i.e., the windshield, both door pillars, the back light (window), etc.

All automobiles experience a negative interior pressure or slight vacuum when in motion. As the air flows over the automobile, the moving air over the car is of a lower pressure than air that is not moving. This is the same principle that occurs when air moves over an airplane wing resulting in lower pressure on the top of the wing than on the bottom creating lift. Since automobiles are not air tight, the design must accommodate this condition, trapping the water that is included in the incoming air for ventilation. The Corvette design was adequate in this respect, but door and window sealing was lacking, resulting in water leaks into the passenger compartment. We did not use the vacuum test booth much because almost all Corvettes, especially convertibles, leaked in that test.

The vacuum booth was like the static booth but was equipped with a large vacuum hose that was placed in the drivers window. The driver rolled the window down, placed the vacuum hose and its adapter in the opening and ran the test. The water test was initiated by the driver turning on the headlamps which turned on the water test that ran for a prescribed time, 4 minutes, minimum. I rode with the inspector that conducted the test many times. There was no interior trim in the job so we sat on boxes. My first End of Month Water Test report is shown in Image 18.

I was able to get the average leaks per job down to about 1 per job as time went along. Assembly line worker turnover and work load were major issues contributing to water leaks. As I stated earlier, each operator work cycle was about 10 minutes requiring an assembler to remember many tasks and attend many details.

INTER-ORGANIZATION LETTERS ONLY
CHEVROLET

TO	K. F. Brooks	ADDRESS:	Chevrolet-St. Louis
FROM	L. M. Galloway	ADDRESS:	Chevrolet-St. Louis
SUBJECT	Corvette Water Leaks	DATE:	July 29, 1963

During the period of July 1 through July 22, 1963, 1685 Corvettes were water tested resulting in 1939 water leaks. This is an average of 1.15 leaks per unit, a decrease of 0.09 leaks since July 16, 1963.

The most frequent Corvette water leak as of this date occurs at the aero coupe door rear drain gutter. Investigation of this area during the first shift, July 22, 1963, revealed a small opening remaining between the cab frame and the drain gutter where the front drain gutter is brazed to the rear gutter reinforcement. The instruction manual specifies, in section 1, sheet A14.00, this joint to brazed and metal finished. Foreman L.Webb was notified of this and the operation altered to close this hole. The second shift operation on the same date was observed and it was found that this hole was being closed. According to M. Cary, second shift foreman, this hole has been closed on second shift for an undetermined length of time.

Inspection of the completed cab frame on the first shift, July 22, 1963, before the application of Plastisol sealer, part number 3813662, to the drain gutter revealed an excess of spot weld sealer, part number 3809224, in the rear lower end of the drain gutter. The spot weld sealer, when heated, gives off gasses causing the Plastisol sealer to crack and thus give route to possible water leaks. This was brought to production L. Webb's attention. According to second shift foreman, M. Cary, the second shift has reduced the spot weld sealer in this area to a minimum to improve this condition.

During the period of July 1 through July 17, 1963, 128 Corvettes were water tested in a static-vacuum water test booth. Due to equipment availability, hardtop equipped models were not vacuum tested. The results of this test, which was conducted on completer units ready for shipment, is shown in the following data.

128 units static tested show 32, or 25% O.K. units.

57 units vacuum tested show 24, or 42% O.K. units.

	Static		Vacuum	
Defect	Number defective	Percent Defective	Number Defective	Percent Defective
Bottom Door Trim R	75	58.5	28	49.0
Bottom Door Trim L	29	22.6	7	12.3
Bottom Windshield Garnish Mldg. R	7	5.5	5	8.8
Bottom Windshield Garnish Mldg. L	12	9.4	7	12.3
Bottom W/Seal to W/Shield Gutter R	8	6.2	10	17.3
Bottom W/Seal to W/Shield Gutter L	10	7.3	15	26.4
Bottom of Back Glass R	1	0.8	5	8.8
Bottom of Back Glass L	3	2.3	6	10.5

Image 18

The assembly workers were really good guys. (No females in the plant at that time.) I asked a body shop operator to bond a small scrap of fiberglass to the inner door in an effort to deflect water away from a leaking area. He did it gladly for about a week and I could see no improvement so I told him he could stop. He said, "Thats okay, I don't mind, it might help a little so I will keep putting the part on." I was taken aback with his desire to contribute and he kept putting the part on, how long I do not know.

I have a lot of memories of Corvette launch and production that I cannot share here. Most are good memories of good friends doing their best.

The following is from a hand written memo to my supervisor, John Turek.

❖ *Subject: My 1964 Corvette Quality Accomplishments*

❖ *During the year beginning January 1, 1964 and ending December 31, 1964, I used my time improving the Corvette body.*

❖ *I spent 115 days, of which 4 were Saturdays, in the DowSmith Ionia plant assisting them with their start of production problems and later with quality improvement. Contact of this source has been my largest consumer of time establishing a quality level and advising them of the necessity of maintaining that level.*

❖ *On July 8 th I was assigned to the Corvette Improvement Program Committee which ended in January 1965. I spent 60 days in St. Louis on this and other varied assignments.*

❖ *Office time consumed 43 days of my time in 1964 writing reports, investigating design, etc.*

❖ *The Quality Control Classes and Seminars in Flint took 12 days.*

❖ *The contacting of Findlay Industries (Corvette seat and convertible top supplier) in Findlay Ohio required 6 days.*

❖ *Molded Fiberglass Body Contacts required 6 days.*

❖ *Door trim corrective action at Mitchell-Bentley in Owosso, Mich. required 5 days.*

❖ *Carpet approval at the J. P. Stevens Co. in Greenville, S.C. required two trips to that source 4 days.*

MY 1965 CORVETTE

I bought a 1965 Corvette Coupe, in the spring of 1964. It is serial number 194375S106225, body number 971 and order number 15901. The photo on the cover is my Corvette.

I am not sure what my motivation was at the time, perhaps it was the many friendships that I developed in Ionia, but I specified that the body of my Corvette be built in Ionia. I was following the job, my Corvette body, down the assembly line. As I approached the operator assembling the door glass and window lift regulator into the door it was obvious he was having difficulty. I ask how it was going as I frequently did upon visiting assemblers. He exclaimed, "I pity the poor slob who buys this job". I said, "This is my Corvette." Most of the operators knew me, seemed to like me, and knew I was having my Corvette body built in Ionia. He looked at me for a second and dropped the parts onto the floor of the body and said, "Oh hell, we're going to finish the build of this job off line."

When my Corvette body came off line in Ionia, several selected assemblers took most of the trim out of the job and carefully replaced it. It looked great, especially after the special treatment on the Glenn Green paint job.

Additionally, there is a bond joint between the underbody and the roof panel that runs along over the rear wheels and across the body under the back lite (rear window). This joint sometimes distorts the surface of the roof because of the exothermic heat of the bond material. A special, more expensive, bond material that did not produce exothermic heat was used on my Corvette to reduce and nearly eliminate this distortion.

When my "special" Corvette body arrived in St. Louis, I was there. The St. Louis assembly plant management met me and introduced me to my new Corvette. I was very pleased and my St. Louis friends were proud. I told them that I wanted the body built in Ionia used to build my Corvette. I thought that my Corvette body was probably in the system. I knew the body number of the body built in Ionia and upon checking the inventory, sure enough, my special body was waiting on the conveyor, in the basement of the Corvette Plant, to be married to a chassis. The St. Louis management was disappointed but agreeable.

I do not recall feeling any remorse. Perhaps I should have. I do remember part of the reason I specified an Ionia built body. I wanted to demonstrate to the St. Louis management that I believed the Ionia Team was just as good at building Corvette bodies as was the St. Louis Team. I dealt with a lot of suppliers to Chevrolet and always felt that Chevrolet took advantage of the suppliers because they could. Siding with suppliers was not a popular position for me.

I sold my Corvette in 1966 just before moving to South America. The paint was fading a little so I drove it to Ionia and showed it to the DowSmith Management. They asked me if I could leave it there for a few days while they repainted it. I agreed and in a few days I had a new paint job.

The Corvette Quality Liaison assignment was a high point in my work experience and one that I cherish to this day. I made a lot of really good friends, most are likely deceased by now. I went back to

St. Louis recently and the old Corvette plant is gone and the last time I passed by the Ionia plant it was gone. Quite different than my first visit to Ionia when they had a 1963 Buick Riviera in their front yard as a monument to their contribution to that car.

During the Summer of 1966, I applied for a position with General Motors Overseas Operations and was promoted to Quality Control Manager, GM De Venezuela, S.A., General Motors South America, Caracas, Venezuela. Before leaving Detroit, my co-workers presented me a few gifts and a certificate, Image 19 along with several small pieces of Corvette carpet that I had received in the approval process. My responsibility included color matching and approval of supplier samples.

Suppliers of parts to Chevrolet were required to submit a sample of their part for inspection to Chevrolet Central Office Quality Control for approval before they received a release for shipment to the assembly plants. Purchasing could not pay the supplier without this approval.

My co-workers also issued a Sample Inspection Report to me, Image 20. Inspected by signers are Fred Chall, Bruce Boyle, C. L. Taylor, Herb Korth, Paul Hill and Barb Henry; Approved by John Turek, my supervisor and Jim Steen, John's supervisor, co-workers and friends.

THE FOLLOWING PRESENTATION IS BEING AWARDED TO YOU IN HOPES THAT IT CAN SERVE AS A TYPICAL EXAMPLE OF YOUR ABILITY TO PROVIDE THE CHEVROLET CORVETTE WITH ITS FIRST MOLDED CARPET INTERIOR. WITH ALL RESPECTS FOR YOUR HONEST AND SINCERE EFFORTS TO RAISE CHEVROLET STANDARDS, IT IS OUR INTENTION THAT THESE SAMPLES WILL ENABLE YOU TO ESTABLISH YOURSELF AS A GMOO MOLDED CARPET EXPERT IN CARACAS.

THANK YOU FOR YOUR DUTIFUL SERVICE.

BODY AND FRAME GROUP

Image 19

CHEV 107
REV. 2-65

CHEVROLET - CENTRAL OFFICE

DIVISION OF GENERAL MOTORS CORPORATION
GENERAL MOTORS BUILDING

DETROIT, MICHIGAN 48202

SAMPLE INFORMATION

PART NO. __XXX-XX-XXXX__

PART NAME __L. M. Galloway__

SOURCE __Mr. and Mrs. R. A. Galloway__

__Corvette Quality Contact Man__

QUANTITY __1 Only__

DATE RECEIVED __4-29-36__
BLUE PRINT DATE __7-29-35__
WEIGHT __OVER__
TRADE MARK __GOLD WATCH CHAIN__

DATE INSPECTED __22 August 1966__
LAB. WORK ORDER __Charge to GMOO__
INSPECTED BY __Body and Frame Group__
RECOMMENDATION __See Below__

FULLY APPROVED	REJECTED	PROVISIONALLY APPROVED FOR CHEVROLET REQUIREMENTS	INCOMPLETE PENDING FURTHER CHECKS
	X		

THIS IS BASED ON THE SAMPLE STATUS SHOWN BELOW:

DIMENSIONALLY O.K.	DIMENSIONALLY INCORRECT	REJECTED FOR COLOR OR APPEARANCE	PENDING LABORATORY	SOURCE TO NOTE ATTACH. LAB. REPORT	ADD. SAMPLES NOT REQUIRED	CORRECTED SAMPLES REQUIRED
X	X			X	X	

REMARKS

* DENOTES DISCREPANCIES WHICH MUST BE CORRECTED ON ALL PRODUCTION SHIPMENTS.

Dimensional Requirements:

    Skis too short (Verified by limp)
    Boots too warm
    Foot too heavy (Verified by police report)

Color Requirements:

    Too tan during winter months

Lab Requirements:

    Traces of attraction to opposite sex in excess of maximum specifications

NOTE: Additional samples not required as we are cancelling this part as a
       Chevrolet requirement due to sources refusing to produce more
       samples.

FINAL DISPOSITION: Carefully crate and ship to Caracas, Attention:
                GMOO Division, for their evaluation and use.

INSPECTED BY: _[signatures]_

APPROVED BY: _[signatures]_

Image 20

ACKNOWLEDGMENT

I consider myself very fortunate to have been afforded the opportunity to begin my automotive career with Chevrolet Division of General Motors Corporation and especially working on Corvette in St. Louis, Missouri. My promotion to Chevrolet Central Office Quality Control in Detroit was especially fortunate. Those years paved the way for me within General Motors and with the opportunities that came my way afterwards.

My life long career in Quality Control began on August 16, 1962 and continued through 1998. I met W. Edwards Deming and Joseph M. Juran, both recognized as major contributors and sometimes evangelist in the field of Quality. I learned that the greatest accomplishment and pleasure derived from a career in Quality depended largely on the joy derived from helping others achieve their ambitions.

I managed the Quality functions in many organizations and always enjoyed helping others and watching and watching them succeed.

INDEX

Printed in the United States
by Baker & Taylor Publisher Services